Praise

'Jules Love has written the playbook every agency leader needs right now. After building and selling three agencies whilst navigating every tech wave from web 1.0 to blockchain, I know what separates successful technology adoption from expensive experiments. *Shift - AI For Agencies* provides agency leaders the concrete steps they need to turn AI from a threat into competitive advantage.'
— **Mary Keane-Dawson**, Chair of BIMA

'As someone working at the frontline of AI adoption in a creative agency, I found this book both grounding and energising. Jules captures exactly what many of us are wrestling with: how to move beyond experiments into real, structured change. It's rare to find something that speaks with this much clarity and practicality about the creative sector's future. For me, it feels less like a book and more like a companion for the road ahead.'
— **Jason Anderson**, Digital Director, Avantgarde

'Leveraging AI in an environment as complex as the modern marketing agency is extremely difficult – I can personally attest to this. Jules breaks down exactly where and how you can use AI to start adding value. It's a must read for agency owners who are wrestling with these changes.'
— **Kate Ross**, Founder and CEO of eight&four

'It's one of the best work-related books I've read in years – well-written, to-the-point and packed with practical, must-do-now ideas for furthering your career and safeguarding your business.'
— **Simon Bates**, Creative Director, TMP

'*Shift - AI For Agencies* is the playbook agencies need right now. Jules is without question one of the leading voices in the agency and AI space, and he doesn't just explain AI, he shows how to make it part of your creative DNA. Clear, practical and inspiring, this is essential reading for any agency leader navigating the changes needed to future proof your agency.'
— **Spencer Gallagher**, Founder of Bluhalo
  and Author of *Agencynomics*

'What sets *Shift - AI For Agencies* apart is Jules Love's understanding that AI adoption is fundamentally about people, not technology. The book addresses the real barriers agencies face – time constraints, skill gaps, client concerns and cultural resistance – with practical solutions that actually work. This is essential reading for any agency leader who wants to harness AI's power while preserving their team's creative spirit.'
— **Steve Turner**, Co-Founder of mark-making*

'Jules Love's *Shift - AI For Agencies* isn't just another book about AI; it's the definitive field guide for leaders navigating the biggest shift in creative work since the internet itself. For agencies grappling with how to redefine their impact and unlock new frontiers of creative value, this is an essential read.'
— **Ant Hill**, Principal Consultant GenAI, Google Cloud

'At Mr B & Friends we've always believed in challenging the ordinary. This book makes it clear how AI can help your team push boundaries further than ever before. It's not about becoming an "AI agency," it's about becoming a better version of the agency you already are.'
— **Simon Barbato**, Founder & CEO, Mr B & Friends

AI FOR AGENCIES

LEAD YOUR TEAM THROUGH THE BIGGEST SHIFT SINCE DIGITAL

JULES LOVE

Rethink

First published in Great Britain in 2025
by Rethink Press (www.rethinkpress.com)

© Copyright Julian Love

All rights reserved. No part of this publication may be reproduced, stored in or introduced into a retrieval system, or transmitted, in any form, or by any means (electronic, mechanical, photocopying, recording or otherwise) without the prior written permission of the publisher.

The right of Julian Love to be identified as the author of this work has been asserted by him in accordance with the Copyright, Designs and Patents Act 1988.

This book is sold subject to the condition that it shall not, by way of trade or otherwise, be lent, resold, hired out, or otherwise circulated without the publisher's prior consent in any form of binding or cover other than that in which it is published and without a similar condition including this condition being imposed on the subsequent purchaser.

Contents

Preface	1
PART 1 A Transformational Shift	3
1 **Introduction**	5
The structure of this book	9
2 **Why creative agencies are at the eye of the AI storm, and what to do about it**	13
The road to generative AI	14
How generative AI works	18
Algorithmic intelligence	20
Key takeaways	23

3 How agencies and brands are using AI — 25

The networks — 26
The campaigns that mark a turning point — 29
Key takeaways — 34

4 What can I do with AI? — 37

Imagination is more important than knowledge — 38
Research that sets you apart — 39
From data to strategic direction — 40
Visual territories and creative exploration — 42
Content creation and scaling — 43
Campaign development and execution — 44
The operational backbone — 45
Making it real for your clients — 46
Great ideas there, but what tools should I use? — 47
Key takeaways — 49

5 How to speak AI — 51

1. Thinking: Don't switch off your brain — 52
2. Prompting: Your new creative language — 55
3. Informing: Everything is now data — 65
Creating custom AI assistants — 68
AI assistants in action — 72
Key takeaways — 78

6 Working with image generators — 81
Why this changes everything — 82
Choosing your creative weapons — 83
Mastering the art of AI direction — 86
Beyond still images: The moving picture — 89
The real-world revolution — 90
Key takeaways — 91

7 Data privacy, IP and ethics — 95
Is this stuff legal? — 95
The free tier trap — 97
Copyright in the AI era: Who owns what? — 99
What this means for your work — 101
Be careful what you mimic — 102
Bias and the illusion of neutrality — 103
The environmental reality check — 106
Key takeaways — 110

PART 2 Building Your AI Strategy — 113

8 The journey to AI maturity — 115
The four stages of AI maturity — 117
So where are you on the journey? — 122
Key takeaways — 123

9 Vision and strategy — 127

- Understanding your agency's DNA — 128
- Moving beyond deliverables to value — 130
- Why this matters for AI adoption — 131
- The AI Strategy Canvas™ — 132
- The implications of the AI Strategy Canvas for your business — 136
- From big ideas to specific projects — 138
- Prioritising your initiatives: The 3S Framework — 141
- Measuring success: Defining some metrics for AI initiatives — 143
- Start building your AI roadmap — 146
- Making your roadmap work — 146
- Key takeaways — 148

10 People, skills and culture — 151

- Assembling your AI taskforce — 152
- Identifying key members and their responsibilities — 153
- Developing an AI adoption charter — 156
- Setting the taskforce up for success — 157
- Cultivating an AI-forward culture — 158
- Encouraging experimentation — 160

Implementing a buddy system 161
Fostering ownership 163
Creating shared moments 164
Address specific fears with specific responses 166
Integrating AI into development
and recruitment 167
Investing in AI skills and knowledge 168
Create a custom AI skills matrix 172
Training formats that actually work 172
Creating AI learning journeys 175
Making it stick: Beyond the initial enthusiasm 177
Key takeaways 178

11 Data and tools   181

Everything is now data 182
Making your data work for you 184
How to structure your data for AI 186
Collecting the data you need 188
Connecting AI to your digital workspace 189
Embedding AI into your workflows 192
Building your prompt library:
The knowledge multiplier 197
Key takeaways 198

12	**Governance and accountability**	**201**
	Governance: What's important to your clients	202
	Building an AI policy	203
	Communicating with clients	206
	When clients say no	210
	The £50,000 question	212
	Accountability: Keeping your roadmap on track	215
	Building for the future	220
	Key takeaways	221
13	**Where is all this going?**	**225**
	Beyond faster and cheaper	226
	Your new celebrity workforce	227
	The age of personal AI assistants	228
	Three roads diverging	229
	From campaigns to creative engines	230
	The death of the project-based model	231
	Your org chart is obsolete	232
	The Netflix test	233
	Becoming the creative director of everything	234
	What this means for your agency	235

Postscript: How I used AI to help me write this book	**239**
Notes	**243**
Acknowledgements	**249**
The Author	**251**

Preface

When I first picked up a camera, I didn't expect it to change how I see the world.

I'd spent eight years as a consultant, advising global brands on marketing and innovation – building strategies in boardrooms where language was rational, tidy and abstract. Then my photography career took off, and suddenly I was halfway up a mountain in the Alps at sunrise, directing a commercial shoot for a global tech client, chasing light, instinct and emotion. Just like that, creativity wasn't a theory anymore, it was something alive. Messy. Magical. Tangible.

That duality – strategy and spontaneity, structure and spark – has shaped everything I've done since.

I've spent over two decades moving between creative and corporate worlds. Whether working with organisations like *The Guardian*, *The Times* and the BBC to help them build digital into their human functions, or shooting world-spanning campaigns for Canon, Samsung, Google and Hilton, I've always been mulling over one question: how do we build systems that don't just allow creativity, but amplify it?

Then generative AI came along, and it was the key that unlocked this future.

Suddenly, we're not just talking about optimising workflows or streamlining operations. We're talking about expanding what it means to be creative. Making the unimaginable possible. Creating tools that collaborate with us – tools that can sketch, write, design, ideate and surprise us. Yet, most of the conversation has been about fear, job loss, control and whether we're replacing the artist with the algorithm.

I don't see it that way.

This book is about rewiring our creative relationship with AI – not just understanding what it does, but exploring what it could mean for how we think, lead and make. It's not a manual (although it is practical). It's a mindset shift (but it's not a self-help book). It's a provocation. A field guide for leaders of creative businesses navigating a fast-changing world.

You'll find tools and frameworks here, stories and strategies and lessons from my work helping over forty creative teams reimagine how they use AI. More than that, though, I hope you'll find permission – permission to play, experiment and lead without having all the answers.

Because the truth is, none of us do.

But if we get this right – if we lean into the unknown with clarity, creativity and courage – AI won't diminish our creativity, it'll deepen it.

Let's begin.

PART 1
A Transformational Shift

1
Introduction

AI has been around for a long time. It helps recommend products on Amazon or suggest new shows you might like on Netflix. It sits behind the facial recognition on your iPhone. It filters out the spam in your email inbox, and helps you find that photo of your grandmother on your computer. It sets the prices of your airline tickets.

Generative AI, however, is relatively new. For the first time, computers can do more than classify content or predict future trends based on your past behaviour. They can generate new content from scratch and actually simulate human thinking.

The first time I tried ChatGPT, back in January 2023, it was hard not to be amazed. This was version 3.5, the first released to the public. Here, for the first time, a powerful AI model was available to anyone with a computer. No longer did you need a computer science degree or a machine-learning doctorate to play with AI. You just needed to be able to type in English. The barrier to accessing powerful AI tools had suddenly dropped from sky high to zero.

Since then we have already seen tremendous advances in the technology. Firstly, the language models have simply got better. ChatGPT has moved from 3.5 to 4 to 4o to 4.5 – and as I proofread this manuscript, OpenAI have just announced GPT5. Meanwhile, Microsoft have launched Copilot, Google have released Gemini and Anthropic have created Claude. In the last year we have gone beyond chatbots to reasoning models like GPT5, Claude 4 and Gemini 2.5 Pro, and the models continue to show significant improvements every few months.

They haven't just become better, though, they have also become multi-modal – they can now understand not only text, but also images, data, voice, video and more. OpenAI building image generation into ChatGPT 4o created a moment even more viral as its initial launch, boosting their number of weekly users to over 800 million.

Not only that, but you can now speak to your model in real time in something that is increasingly close to a human conversation. It can digest your documents and turn them into an engaging podcast with extremely natural sounding voices. It can generate pictures, infographics and design elements at a speed no designer can match.

The pace of improvement of these tools is astonishing, and the creative industries are the canaries in the coal mine in terms of how these tools will impact the world of work. Writing copy and creating visual imagery goes to the heart of how we deliver value to our clients. What does it mean once computer models can perform a task as well as the average human? Is it the end of creativity as we know it? Does it mean the downfall of the creative sector? Are the days of running a design agency or advertising agency over?

The answer is no, and I'll explain why later, but to thrive requires embracing AI and building it into the way your agency works. Adopting AI isn't a switch you can flip, it requires a deliberate transformation. This book will show you not just why you need to change, but also how to do it.

Artificial Intelligence isn't just another technology trend – it's becoming as fundamental to creative professionals as digital was twenty-five years ago, and the impact will be felt not just in our industry, but across the whole of the economy and society, too.

You're likely already using AI in some form, perhaps tentatively exploring what it can do for your business. However, the truth is, AI will soon be as essential to your workflow as email, design software and search engines.

Marketing departments of brands are under continuous pressure to do more with less. Ten years ago, the average marketing budget was 12.5% of sales, while today it is 7.5%.[1] In that time, the number of assets they need to generate to power their campaigns has gone from thirty a year to over 3,000, as highly tailored, short-lived social content has become a key marketing channel.

Today's challenges – tight budgets, rising client expectations and intense competition – make the adoption of AI not just a choice, but a necessity for many brands. The technology companies know this. Google and Meta are selling AI-enabled platforms directly to brands, while platforms like Pencil from

Brandtech put AI-driven campaign development, asset generation and evaluation in the hands of clients.

Meanwhile, we're seeing traditional search engines and AI collide, with Google now producing AI overviews that dramatically reduce the number of click throughs, and ChatGPT beginning to suggest eCommerce links directly in its chat results. The impact this will have on content marketing and eCommerce are hard to predict, but it will have a profound impact on the services that agencies in this space need to provide.

I studied Applied Generative AI at MIT, then co-founded Spark AI to help agencies navigate the future. We were supported by Innovate UK to build our AI Accelerator programme, built on insights from thirty independent agencies. This book contains everything we have learned over the last eighteen months spent working with more than forty agencies to build AI into the way they work, future proof their business models and redefine their relationships with their clients.

This book is your practical guide to not just surviving, but thriving in this AI-enabled future. It doesn't matter if you're a small independent agency or a global network – the core principles remain the same. The agencies that understand how to harness AI strategically will outpace those that either ignore it or implement it without a clear vision.

In the pages that follow, I'll share insights from the frontline of AI adoption in creative agencies. You'll learn how to move from experimentation to strategic implementation, how to upskill your team, and most importantly, how to maintain your creative edge while taking advantage of these powerful new tools.

Make no mistake, your creative edge remains your most valuable asset. As you'll discover, AI isn't a wholesale replacement for human creativity, but it will change and amplify it in ways we're only just beginning to understand.

In this book, I'm going to argue that, while AI tools like ChatGPT and Midjourney are certainly going to disrupt our industry – and eventually almost every other industry too – there is still a huge amount of value in the skills and knowledge we have accumulated. In fact, I'll go as far to say I think there will be more creative jobs in the future than there have ever been. However, to remain relevant, we will need to change the way we work, change the kind of work we do, and change the way we charge for that work.

As we go through this book, I'll explain what these new tools are all about, how the big, networked agencies are leveraging them, and how, as an independent agency, you can too. We'll talk about how to build an AI strategy that differentiates you in the marketplace, how you can leverage the opportunities generative AI creates through automation, augmentation and innovation, how you can drive adoption at your agency, and finally where this is all going and what the agency of the future will look like.

The structure of this book

Think of this book as a practical field guide to the AI revolution that's already reshaping our industry. I've divided it into two parts that mirror the journey every agency needs to take.

Part 1: What you need to know about AI

This isn't another theoretical deep-dive into machine-learning algorithms. It's the practical stuff that matters to you as a creative professional. You'll discover what generative AI actually is and why agencies are among the first industries to feel its impact. I'll show you how the big networks and major brands are already deploying AI, and what that means for your competitive position. Most importantly, you'll learn exactly how to use these tools effectively, from getting brilliant results out of ChatGPT to creating compelling visuals with image generators.

We'll also tackle the thorny questions you're probably wrestling with already: data privacy, intellectual property, bias and environmental impact. No corporate-speak here – just straight answers to help you make informed decisions.

Part 2: Building your AI strategy

Here's where we get serious about transformation. You'll learn how to think like an AI pioneer, moving beyond scattered experiments to strategic implementation. I'll walk you through creating an AI strategy that actually works – one that builds on your agency's existing strengths rather than trying to turn you into a technology company. You'll discover how to build an AI-forward culture, develop the right skills in your team, and treat your data like the strategic asset it is. We'll explore how to embed AI into your workflows systematically, get governance right without killing innovation, and – crucially – how to talk to clients about all this without undermining your value. Finally, we'll look ahead. Where is this all going? What will the agency of the future look like? How do you position yourself to thrive rather than merely survive?

Each chapter provides practical advice and actionable steps to help you lead your agency into the AI age. This isn't just another book about AI. It's a roadmap for agency leaders ready to embrace change. As I have said, this book is a guide to thriving, not just surviving, in the new AI era. Let's begin this journey together.

2
Why creative agencies are at the eye of the AI storm, and what to do about it

You might be thinking a chapter explaining what generative AI is would be redundant today, when AI tools are seemingly everywhere around us. However, to truly grasp AI's significance, we need to understand how it works, what it is good at, and what it is bad at. Generative AI – or GenAI – is unlike any other form of computer use we have experienced, and to get the most out of it requires fundamentally changing the way we think about and interact with computers.

It also points the way to its implications for the creative industry. In this chapter, we'll uncover what generative AI is, how it works and why it's reshaping the landscape for agencies and brands alike.

For the last twenty years, whenever we have been faced with a plain white screen and a text box, it has been a search engine. Now, it is likely to be a large language model (LLM – the collective term for models such as ChatGPT), but the way they operate under the hood, and how we get value from a search engine and an LLM are fundamentally different.

For many of us, it seems like AI exploded onto the scene at the end of 2022, when OpenAI released ChatGPT 3.5 as a consumer product. The reality is it's been a long time coming. How did we get here?

The road to generative AI

The emergence of generative AI is the result of three converging trends over the last fifty years: advancements in modelling techniques, exponential growth in computing power, and an unprecedented abundance of data. Together, these forces have propelled AI from a niche research field into a transformative technology that's set to reshape the modern world. Let's look at each of these more closely.

Modelling techniques

Research into AI and machine intelligence is almost as old as the computer itself. Back in the 1950s, pioneering researchers such as John McCarthy and Marvin Minsky began to talk about machines that could perform tasks requiring 'intelligence'.[2]

Back then, getting computers to perform useful tasks relied on creating hardcoded rules and logic. Computers could solve problems if – and only if – they were given explicit instructions on how to solve them. It's as if you had to write the rule book for every problem, and every problem required its own rule book. This approach, known as Symbolic AI, could work reasonably well for problems like chess, where the rules and logic are clear and explicit, but it quickly struggled with the complexities of real-world applications – and a model with rules for one problem couldn't hope to solve a problem from a different field.

The 1980s brought about a new approach: machine learning, which allowed computers to learn patterns from data instead of following strict instructions. Instead of programmers hand-coding rules, machines could begin to calculate the rules for themselves.

Machine learning powered IBM's Deep Blue when it beat the reigning chess world champion Gary Kasparov in 1997, and Google Deepmind's AlphaGo when it beat Lee Sedol, the world's best Go player, in 2016. However, while AI models by this point excelled at classification (what is this a picture of?) and prediction (what's the next best move?), until this point, AI models couldn't create anything new.

The real breakthrough for generative AI came in 2017 with the introduction of the transformer model, detailed in a now-famous paper 'Attention is all you need', written by eight researchers at Google.[3] Transformers introduced a new concept called self-attention, which allowed models to analyse relationships between different parts of a dataset – like words in a sentence or pixels in an image. Unlike older models, which processed sequences step-by-step, transformers could consider all elements at once, making them faster and more accurate.

Transformers have become the backbone of generative AI, powering tools like ChatGPT. In fact, the GPT in ChatGPT stands for Generative Pre-trained Transformer. These models don't just process information, they generate entirely new content – text, images, music and more – that, at its best, feels human-made.

Computing power

None of these advances in model building would have been possible without huge strides in computing power. AI research has largely been constrained by the limits of computing. In the past, training even a simple model required weeks of processing on expensive hardware, while more ambitious ideas remained locked in the realm of the theoretical. However, ever since the 1950s, computer chips have got faster and faster, roughly doubling in processing power every eighteen months (named Moore's Law after Intel's co-founder), but, ultimately, they could still only process one task at a time.[4]

That changed with the adoption of graphics processing units (GPUs), first developed in the 1990s, and originally designed for rendering video game graphics. GPUs turned out to be perfect for the parallel computations required to train large neural networks. Nvidia, one of the leading GPU manufacturers, spotted the trend early and in the mid-2010s bet heavily on optimising their chips for AI.

By the early 2020s, Nvidia was designing and building the chips powering every foundational language model in existence, and as a result has seen their market capitalisation grow ten-fold in three years to become one of the world's most valuable companies. This enormous leap in computing power means that models can now be trained on billions of parameters in weeks, rather than years.

Data

The final piece of the jigsaw is data. Machine-learning systems can only ever be as good as the data they're trained on. In the 1980s, machine learning relied on human-made annotations of chess games to learn from. Then, in the 2000s, people began to build larger labelled datasets like ImageNet to train their models. Millions of pictures were tagged by teams of humans describing what the pictures contained, so machines could learn what was what. However, the digital era has created an absolute flood of it. Today we live our lives online, and every social media post shared, blog post written or video streamed contributes to a growing ocean of information. Generative AI models draw on vast datasets scraped from the internet (a controversial issue which we'll touch on later), capturing the breadth of human knowledge, creativity and conversation.

The perfect storm

Generative AI is therefore the product of a perfect storm: advanced techniques like transformers, hardware that delivers unparalleled processing power, and a virtually limitless supply of data. These trends have fed into each other, creating a feedback loop of progress. Transformers wouldn't have been possible without the computing power to train them. That power would have been meaningless without enough data to feed into the models. All the data in the world wouldn't matter without the right modelling techniques to make sense of it.

Together, these forces have given rise to generative AI as we know it: tools that can write essays, design graphics, compose music and even engage in conversations that feel human. It's no exaggeration to say that this combination of trends will impact every industry it touches. The pace of change is only accelerating.

How generative AI works

To understand how LLMs work, let's start with what they aim to do: mimic human language in a way that feels natural, insightful and, most importantly, useful. Whether they're writing an email, summarising a report or even brainstorming ideas, these systems are designed to produce coherent, relevant text that fits the context of the request.

How does a machine achieve this? The answer lies in a clever combination of mathematics, data and an underlying structure inspired by the way we process information.

Until machine learning came along, every computer programme you have ever used encoded rules that were written by a human. You give the computer an input, it applies a rule its been given, and gives you an output. It doesn't matter whether you're asking it to multiply by two or rotate a 10,000 pixel image in Photoshop – the computer is applying rules to follow your request and giving you the answer.

When trying to apply this approach to human language, though, the rules are just too complex and nuanced to be able to codify them into a computer programme that could perform at anything other than the most basic level.

Machine learning works in a fundamentally different way. Instead of writing rules, machine learning allows the computer to work them out. Instead of giving it a question and the rules by which to solve it, we give the computer both the questions *and* the answers. The computer is then able to calculate what the rule must have been to get from one to the other. Scale this up far enough and give it enough examples, and computers have been able to calculate the rules of human language in a way that is far more complex and nuanced than any human or team of humans could ever codify.

They're trained on billions of sentences – the entire public internet – and learn patterns in how humans use language. They figure out that 'coffee' is often followed by 'cup' or 'shop', that 'difficult' might be paired with 'decision', and that 'marketing' and 'strategy' frequently go hand in hand. The model learns to calculate what is likely to come next based on everything it's seen before.

But what makes LLMs truly powerful isn't just their training – it's their scale. The 'large' in 'large language model' refers to the sheer number of parameters, or internal calculations, that the model uses to create answers. For reference, GPT-3, released in 2022, has 175 billion parameters, while GPT-4 released in 2024 has over 400 billion. The leading models today are thought to have more than 1 trillion. Each of these parameters contribute a small piece to the puzzle of generating language. The more parameters a model has, the more sophisticated its outputs become.

One of the most remarkable aspects of LLMs is their versatility. In the past, computers were excellent at the individual tasks they were designed for, but were useless at anything outside their immediate domain. You can't use Photoshop to manage your customer relationships, you use a CRM system. IBM's Deep Blue beat Gary Kasparov at chess, but it couldn't play draughts.

Because language touches nearly every part of human activity, these models can be applied to almost any task. They can summarise a dense legal document, draft a blog post, debug code and brainstorm creative ideas. Their outputs are far from perfect – sometimes they misunderstand, go off-topic or produce results that don't quite hit the mark. However, when used thoughtfully, they can be an incredible tool for augmenting human creativity and productivity.

As we grow up, our human brains take a decade or more to fully understand language and use it to express complex thoughts. You might have seen this with your own children, as they first mimic, then experiment and then become confident with speech. Today's LLMs can develop something comparable in only a few weeks of training.

Algorithmic intelligence

With AI being able to create outputs that seem extremely human, it is tempting to think of them as being intelligent, and perhaps they are. However, they don't actually understand language the way we do. They don't have emotions, opinions or intent. They are giant calculating machines that have become excellent at predicting what a good answer to your question probably looks like. What they have is an extraordinary ability to replicate the patterns and structures of human communication. It's not thinking in the way we think – it's using probabilities and patterns to create the illusion of thought.

This distinction is important. Although we refer to these models collectively as 'artificial intelligence', they are not intelligent. At least, not in the way that you and I are. Instead, they are a form of algorithmic intelligence, which, when given enough data, computing power and sophisticated models can simulate human intelligence, and often do so extremely convincingly.

Every time you ask the LLM a question, it is guessing the answer. You've almost certainly heard of hallucinations, the term given to mistakes made by language models. The truth is, the models are *always* hallucinating.[5] The trick is to know when the answer is helpful and when it is not, and what tasks this kind of intelligence is suited to and what it is not.

When you fire up ChatGPT, Claude or Gemini, you are faced with what looks like a familiar interface. The empty screen, free of distractions, with nothing but an empty text box and a flashing cursor looks remarkably like a search engine. Google made their fortune from this. However, when you interact with it, what goes on behind the scenes is completely different.

Google search, along with Bing and other traditional search engines, are deterministic database searches. 'Deterministic' meaning that, if you ask the same question twice, you'll get exactly the same answer. Then, to answer your query, it produces a page of blue links. The crucial difference is that you get to see the different links, choose the one with the most relevant information, and evaluate the sources to decide which you trust. If there are no matches, it will tell you.

When you ask a question of an LLM, you get none of this. Firstly, they are non-deterministic. If you ask the same question twice, you'll get slightly different answers (try it!). Secondly, there is no transparency. You'll always get a keen and enthusiastic answer to your question that is often detailed and relevant – but you have no idea how it calculated that answer, how much it had to 'guess', whether the sources it was trained on are accurate and trustworthy, and whether the information it is giving you is correct or not.

This is the key distinction between a search engine like Google and an LLM like ChatGPT or Gemini. Search engines are brilliant tools for facts, for finding documents and sources, and finding the truth when there is only one correct answer. Think of queries such as:

- 'What's the size of the non-alcoholic beer market in the USA in 2025?'
- 'What are the regulations on GDPR in the UK?'
- 'Which sustainable fashion brand has the largest market share?'

In each case there's a single, verifiable answer that a search index can fetch instantly, cite and display. LLMs, on the other hand, are brilliant when there is no single correct answer and instead there are many different ways to give a good answer. So, while law practices, hospitals and financial firms are struggling to harness the power of LLMs, many marketing and creative tasks are perfectly suited to this approach. For example:

- Brainstorming campaign concepts and pushing out twenty rough routes in minutes instead of hours
- Drafting on-brand copy for emails, landing pages or product descriptions that keep the right tone of voice but offer dozens of stylistic variations
- Reworking social media posts for different audiences, lengths or platforms without losing the core idea

- Using interview notes to see how a customer or client might react to your idea, so the team can sanity-check positioning before the research budget arrives

- Turning strategy decks into visual storyboards that help clients 'see' the thinking before a designer ever opens Figma

Combine the power of LLMs with diffusion models that can generate images, sound and video, and it's clear the creative industries – who make their living from creating text and imagery – sit at the eye of the generative AI storm.

Key takeaways

- AI has been around for decades, but generative AI has only been in the public realm since ChatGPT and Midjourney launched in 2022.

- Generative AI models rely on sophisticated modelling techniques, huge amounts of computing power, and the vast amounts of human-created data on the internet.

- LLMs work by predicting patterns, not looking up facts – they calculate what a good answer probably looks like based on training data, making them brilliant for creative tasks but unreliable when there's only one correct answer.

- This variability is what makes them perfectly suited to creative and marketing tasks, and why our industry is the first to feel the impact of generative AI.

- The pace of improvement shows no signs of slowing – with billions being invested and new breakthroughs emerging monthly, today's limitations are tomorrow's solved problems.

Your action point: AI is always guessing

Spend thirty minutes experimenting with ChatGPT or Gemini to experience firsthand how these tools work differently from search engines. Try asking both creative questions ('Generate five campaign concepts for a sustainable fashion brand') and factual questions ('What's the exact population of Manchester in 2024?'). Notice how confident and detailed the responses sound regardless of whether the AI is creating or potentially guessing. This exercise will give you an intuitive understanding of where these tools excel and where you need to be cautious – knowledge that's essential for using them effectively in client work.

3
How agencies and brands are using AI

Consumer attention spans are shortening. Channels are proliferating. The sheer volume of assets that companies need is exploding, while marketing budgets are shrinking. In November 2024, I attended Contagious London, the annual advertising conference where brands and their agencies show off some of the most impactful campaigns for the year. Ipsos showed some revealing statistics. Over the last decade, the average marketing budget of a global CPG brand has shrunk from 12% of sales to 7.5%.[6] Meanwhile, the number of assets they need to generate to drive a campaign has exploded from thirty to 3,500. This combination of media and audience fragmentation is driving asset proliferation, which in turn drives targeting complexity. When put against a background of shrinking budgets you can see how this creates a real challenge for CMOs. It's no surprise that many are looking to AI to help solve this challenge. How are agencies and brands responding?

In this chapter, we'll explore how the big network agencies are deploying AI, how some of their clients are using it, and what this means for brands and their creative work in the near future. From large network agencies to smaller mid-tier firms, the drive to incorporate AI is redefining creativity and client engagement. As these organisations experiment with AI, they are not just adopting new tools, they are laying the groundwork for a radically different way of working.

The networks

You only have to look at the headlines to get a sense that AI is going to change the way that agencies work. In January 2024, Publicis announced it was investing €300 million in building out its internal AI platforms.[7] Their goal? To integrate AI across their entire workflow, from strategy and insights to media planning and creative production. Meanwhile, Omnicom have stated they are trying to automate the entire creative journey from insight generation to campaign evaluation. Not only that, at the start of 2025, Sean Betts, their Chief AI and Innovation Officer, announced the rollout of their AI training programme to all 1,800 employees, with the first stage alone consisting of seven hours of content spanning key skills, ethics and governance. Reassuringly, the topics covered are similar to our AI Fundamentals course we have run with over fifty independents.

But it is WPP, the gorilla of the industry, that has made the biggest investment in AI and is also the one we know the most about, so it's worth diving in to see what's really going on. Stephen Pretorius is the CTO of WPP, and has spent the last several years overseeing the development and deployment of Open, the company's AI platform. Some of the details have been available for a while, but in April 2025, Pretorius was interviewed by Raja Rajamannar, the CMO of Mastercard, as he takes us on a tour of Open.[8] Watching Pretorius talk about Open offers a useful glimpse into where large network agencies are heading, and what independent agencies are competing against.

Rather than using off-the-shelf AI tools, WPP has invested in what they call 'brains' – custom AI models trained on specific client data, brand assets, audience research and strategic guidelines. It's essentially an attempt to codify the institutional knowledge that agencies traditionally hold about their clients.

There's a 'Brand Brain', a custom AI model trained on data, brand assets and details like tone of voice for any given client. Users can then apply the Brand Brain to help ensure adherence to brand guidelines and tone of voice across all content, and to generate a persona, an artificial stand-in for the target audience that can give feedback.

The 'Audience Brain' then analyses detailed demographic, psychographic and behavioural data to provide insights into audience preferences and motivations, to target campaigns. The 'Performance Brain' assesses business and channel performance data to identify what works and direct resources towards the highest-impact activities. Finally, the 'Channel Brain' optimises content for different platforms by analysing past performance metrics and tailoring campaigns to each channel. Alongside the brains sits their AI-powered Production Studio, built with help from Nvidia, allowing them and their clients to generate thousands of visual asset variations with copy in multiple languages.

Rajamannar explains:

> 'When a brand decides it needs an ad for a product it sets off a long and expensive creative process. By the time the ad is served to a potential customer, months have passed, hundreds of people have been involved and often millions of dollars have been spent.'

Open aims to replace some of the most tedious and time-consuming parts of that process.

Pretorius starts the demo by introducing a fictional perfume brand. He takes a Gen Z, eco-conscious consumer as a persona and uses it to create a synthetic focus group, asking it whether it likes the product idea and asking for packaging suggestions. The response the tool gives – maybe a refillable glass bottle and compostable refill bags – won't set the world on fire, but is perhaps a somewhat helpful starting point.

More impressively, he then shows the Content Studio in action. Selecting the audience as one dimension ('eco-conscious Gen Z' or 'trend aware minimalists') and the occasion as the second dimension (eg 'creating a calming bathroom sanctuary', or 'morning hand care routine') Content Studio then quickly generates a visual and call-to-action for each combination – all trained on the brand guidelines stored in the Brand Brain. Pretorius explains that the images are text-to-image generations on a custom-trained model, but the product shots are 3D renders composited onto the AI-generated background.

He then goes on to generate 13,000 visual assets. Looking at the options in the menu bar of the app, it looks like it is possible to select a template for the layout you want to use, the languages you want the copy in, the brand assets you want to show (presumably the 3D renders referenced above) and finally the range of platforms you want to deploy it on. The results are convincing – although I've noticed that, whenever I've seen this demonstrated, it has always been for product photography, suggesting humans may not yet be generated realistically enough for this approach.

Interestingly, the Performance Brain then assigns a predictive score to each asset, suggesting how it will contribute to brand lift, direct response or sales, based on historical performance data and audience research. 'By putting an ad live that has a 30% prediction score versus one with a 70% score, you are sometimes wasting tens of thousands if not hundreds of thousands of dollars,' comments Pretorius.[9]

Watching the demonstration of WPP's Open provides a useful reality check. The platform is clearly sophisticated and represents significant technological advancement. However, it's not magic. It's a systematic application of current AI capabilities to marketing challenges, backed by substantial investment and technical expertise.

The campaigns that mark a turning point

So that's what's going on in the big agencies, but what are brands using it for? While I'm sure almost every brand is using ChatGPT and Copilot to help with campaign ideation, we've seen some big brands clearly deploy AI-generated visuals. Here are a couple that I think are interesting:

Coca-Cola: AI video for advertising

The run up to Christmas 2024 saw Coca-Cola make a splash with an AI re-make of their iconic 'Holidays Are Coming' campaign from the mid-1990s, a series deeply ingrained in popular culture for those of a certain generation (me included).[10]

Launched on YouTube and social channels at the start of November, it was met with a mixture of intrigue and scepticism from the industry. Many people working in advertising and film production immediately lashed out. Criticism ranged from describing the visuals as 'creepy' to a Reddit threat calling them a 'dystopian nightmare', raising questions about whether the execution met audience expectations.[11]

But Coca-Cola was certainly onto something. When tested with general audiences unaware of the campaign's AI origins, the results were overwhelmingly positive. Using System1, a well-known tool for measuring the emotional resonance of advertisements, the campaign scored an impressive 5.9 out of 6, nearly the highest achievable rating.[12] So, despite reservations from industry professionals and nostalgic viewers, the ad certainly resonated with broader audiences.

For those of us interested in the practical applications of AI, the campaign also offered a detailed case study as several of those involved have given interviews. Coca-Cola collaborated with three specialist AI production studios – Secret Level, Silverside AI and Wildcard – and employed an array of tools, including a custom-trained Stable Diffusion model, ChatGPT for storyline development and Silverside's proprietary tool, Director Magic.

Production timelines were remarkably condensed: Silverside delivered a rough draft within three days of the initial briefing, and the final campaign included 110 tailored versions, each featuring unique backgrounds to localise the content to different markets. While AI expedited many aspects of the production, though, it wasn't without its challenges. For instance, the iconic Coca-Cola scripted logo and the signature contour bottle required manual refinement in post-production, reflecting the limitations of current AI tools in handling brand-specific assets. I think this reflects something we're going to see for a while yet, where AI is one part of the whole workflow, rather than standing alone.

Perhaps most interestingly, we're starting to see the production industry changing, with AI-first film studios like Silverside emerging, and AI agencies representing AI artists for brand commissions, rather like we see with photographers and commercial directors today.

Mango: AI imagery for ecommerce

We've also seen Mango, the fashion retailer, publicly lean into AI, using it to create imagery for its ecommerce site. Their initial effort in summer 2024 – a teen-focused summer fashion campaign – was met with mixed reviews. Interestingly, none of the models had their feet showing in the pictures, suggesting they were having difficulty getting them to look realistic. However, by the time Mango produced a teen sport collection in November, the refinement in their AI process was clearly evident. The images look convincing and almost impossible to distinguish from real photography. Importantly, Mango labelled all the photographs as 'generated with AI'.

You might be wondering what consumers make of all this. I checked Mango's Instagram feed after the launch of the sport campaign. The comments were not that the visuals didn't look realistic, or that using AI was somehow unethical. The only negative comments came from potential shoppers concerned their clothing wouldn't fit exactly the same way when it arrived.

Since then, we've seen Hugo Boss delivering AI-generated video of models wearing their latest collection directly onto their ecommerce website, and H&M licensing the likeness of twelve models to allow them to create AI-generated imagery using their appearance. The advantage to H&M? Being able to launch clothing on the website before samples have arrived for a photo shoot, shaving two weeks off their time to market. I'm sure this is just the start of a massive trend for online fashion.

An interesting use of AI in fashion comes from Diarrablu. Founded by a former maths teacher turned Wall Street trader, the brand publishes AI-generated mockups of its new collections on Instagram, and only manufactures the styles their followers indicate are the most popular. The result? Manufacturing directly informed by customer demand, with textile waste reduced by 60%.[13] Founder Diarra Bousso has the job title 'Creative Mathematician' hinting at the blend of creativity and technology at the heart of the company's operations.[14]

Why this means we all have to change

WPP's Open platform and Coca-Cola's Christmas ads are the clearest signs yet that the major agencies and brands aren't just experimenting with AI, they're actually operationalising it. This isn't about shiny tech demos anymore. It's about making their entire global network more consistent, more efficient and more valuable to clients.

For independent agencies, this creates an uncomfortable competitive dynamic. Clients may start expecting the kind of scale and predictive capabilities that only massive technology investments can deliver. Now, you might be thinking, 'Sure, that's fine for WPP or Coca-Cola, but we don't have a global team or a £300M budget'. However, the key lesson to learn from this is that it isn't necessarily about scale; it's about mindset.

As a smaller agency (and, let's face it, compared to WPP, everyone is smaller), you have the flexibility to move quickly. However, speed without structure only gets you so far. Your clients are starting to see what's possible elsewhere. They've had a taste of data-driven decisions, faster turnarounds and platforms that feel custom-built for them. If your processes aren't up to speed, you'll start to feel the pressure – not necessarily because you're less creative, but because you're harder to work with.

You don't need to rebuild an end-to-end platform like Open to compete, but you do need to start exploring how AI can help you build a better workflow. Maybe that means setting up a central workspace for each client, where brand assets, tone of voice and past campaign data live, with a series of custom GPTs that allow you to ideate and interrogate across all those sources.

Maybe it's using AI to generate multiple mockups, build out a brand universe or test creative variations before you even show a client the first draft. Maybe it's rethinking your approval process so client feedback from calls and email threads are automatically captured, the actions categorised and identified, and revisions are completed the same day. We've seen smaller agencies thrive by creating bespoke content hubs for clients, where every campaign is logged, tracked and measurable. Others have built AI-powered brand guardians that flag off-brand copy before it ever gets into a PowerPoint deck.

This is what adaptability looks like. The point isn't to 'keep up with the networks'. It's to stay relevant to your clients – who are already seeing what AI can do for creative collaboration, campaign speed and message precision.

If you're already exploring this, keep going. If you've been waiting for a sign, this is it. You've got the creativity, now it's about building the ways of working that make it scalable. Pretorius's advice is straightforward: 'Start doing things right now. Don't pontificate about it, don't wait, don't watch other people doing it. Get stuck in and start learning by doing.' I couldn't agree more.

Key takeaways

- **The big networks have already placed their bets.** WPP's £300 million annual AI investment and Omnicom's platform rollouts aren't experiments, they're fundamental business transformations happening right now.

- **State-of-the-art technology is democratised.** A £30 monthly ChatGPT subscription gives you access to the same foundational models powering WPP's proprietary platforms.

- **Brands are operationalising AI at scale.** From Coca-Cola's 110 localised Christmas ads to Mango's

AI-generated ecommerce imagery, this isn't future speculation but current reality.

- **Client expectations are shifting rapidly.** They're seeing what's possible elsewhere and will increasingly expect similar capabilities from their agencies.

- **Speed without structure only gets you so far.** Your flexibility as an independent agency is an advantage, but only if you use it to build better workflows, not just move faster.

- **The advantage lies in application, not access.** Everyone can buy the same tools, but knowing how to use them strategically for client challenges is what creates competitive differentiation.

- **This is about enhancing what makes you special.** Successful AI adoption amplifies your existing strengths rather than trying to replicate what the big networks do.

- **Standing still is not an option.** While you don't need to match network-scale investments, you do need to start building AI capabilities before market pressure forces your hand.

> **Your action point: Audit your exposure to AI**
>
> Take twenty minutes to audit what's happening around you. List your three main competitors and research what AI capabilities they're promoting on their websites or LinkedIn. Then identify three clients in your portfolio who might be seeing AI implementations from other suppliers.
>
> Ask yourself: if a prospect compared your agency's AI approach to your competitors' six months from now, would you feel confident in their conclusion? This exercise will clarify whether you're ahead, behind or keeping pace – and help you understand the urgency of your own AI adoption timeline.

4
What can I do with AI?

WPP and the other big networks have deep partnerships with key AI players such as OpenAI, Google and Nvidia. They have also invested hundreds of millions in developing their own platforms. How can smaller independent agencies and brands compete with that? It might seem hopeless. What I'm going to tell you now shows that, actually, there is still everything to play for.

The big secret is that you can access state-of-the-art technology right off the shelf. A $30 subscription to ChatGPT or Microsoft Copilot gets you access to perhaps the most capable LLM in the world right now, and the equal of anything powering WPP Open. If you use Google Workspace, you get access to Gemini practically for free. State-of-the-art technology has never been so easy to access. The catch? You need to know how to use it.

Imagination is more important than knowledge

It's clear that tools like ChatGPT are immensely helpful, but it's not always clear how. It's like opening the box for a piece of IKEA furniture only to find they forgot to include instructions. You can see all the pieces, but it's not obvious how they all fit together and what the outcome looks like. When talking to clients, I often find myself quoting Albert Einstein. In a 1929 interview with the *Saturday Evening Post* about what it took to push forwards the frontiers of physics, he famously said, 'Imagination is more important than knowledge.'[15] I feel this is sometimes the case with generative AI: we have to think outside of our usual ways of working to grasp how we could apply it to our work.

If you're like most creative professionals I've spoken with, you're probably using AI to generate long-form copy or create images. Perhaps you've asked ChatGPT to write social posts or Midjourney to create mood boards. I want to show you that, while these applications certainly have their place, they barely scratch the surface of what's possible.

The real power of AI in creative work doesn't just lie at the end of your process – producing final copy and artwork. It's in the beginning and middle stages where these tools can truly transform how you work. Think about it: what if you could have a thought partner available 24/7 to help you research, brainstorm ideas, test concepts and rapidly prototype? What if you could slash the time spent on low-value tasks like gathering information about your competitors from fifty websites and instead focus more energy on the truly value-adding aspects of your work, like understanding how to position your client in their market? What if you could explore ten creative directions in the time it used to take to explore two?

The key shift here is simple: stop thinking of AI as just another production tool. Start seeing it as your creative partner from day one to project wrap. The best agencies aren't just using AI to speed up their final artwork, they're weaving it through everything they do – client onboarding, research, strategy development, creative exploration, campaign ideation, production support and performance analysis. What does that really look like on a client project? Let's take a look.

Research that sets you apart

Imagine you've just won a pitch for a sustainable fashion brand. In the old world, your first week would be spent frantically Googling competitors, trawling through industry reports and trying to piece together market dynamics. With AI, that research foundation gets built in hours, not days.

Kate Ross, CEO of eight&four, explained how they're transforming this process:

> 'One of our nicest buildouts is for reactive social content. AI has been phenomenal for helping us review large amounts of data across the internet on our brands live – looking at Reddit threads for a credit card brand, for instance, and doing that in real time across our clients' brands plus competitor brands to generate reactive content. That would have taken a lot of time before, and AI has really sped things up.'

Here's how this translates to your sustainable fashion client. You start by asking ChatGPT or Perplexity to research the UK sustainable fashion landscape, identifying major trends, key competitors and opportunities for your brand. Within minutes, you've got a comprehensive overview that includes everything from Patagonia's brand positioning to emerging players like Kotn and Girlfriend Collective.

But you don't stop there. You can ask the AI to analyse Reddit threads about sustainable fashion, extract sentiment from customer reviews of competing brands, and identify gaps in the market that your client might exploit. The AI can process thousands of data points simultaneously – something impossible for a human researcher working through sources one at a time.

For your sustainable fashion brand, this might reveal that, while consumers care about sustainability, they're frustrated by the limited style options in eco-friendly clothing, or that younger consumers are particularly interested in transparency about supply chain practices. These insights become the foundation for everything that follows.

From data to strategic direction

With your research foundation solid, AI becomes your strategic thinking partner. Upload all those customer interview transcripts from your client's previous research, focus group notes and market studies. Ask the AI to identify thematic patterns, surprising insights and potential strategic opportunities. The process is revealing. Instead of spending days manually coding interview responses, you get back a comprehensive analysis highlighting that customers care more about garment longevity than carbon footprint reduction, or that they're willing to pay higher prices but then expect premium quality and design. These aren't obvious insights – they're the kind of strategic goldmines that come from processing vast amounts of qualitative data simultaneously.

Here's where it gets interesting. Instead of accepting the AI's first strategic suggestions, use it as a critical thinking partner. Present your emerging brand positioning and ask it to be rigorous in its critique. Where are the logical flaws? What assumptions might be wrong? How might competitors respond? This process of strategic stress-testing can dramatically strengthen your thinking before it ever reaches the client.

You can take this even further by creating interactive personas based on your target audience research. Instead of static persona documents gathering dust, develop custom AI models that embody different customer types. Your strategists can now 'interview' these personas about potential messaging approaches, pricing strategies or product features. Imagine if a healthcare marketing agency created AI personas representing different patient groups, allowing their strategists to 'interview' these personas about concerns, preferences and reactions to potential messaging approaches. For your sustainable fashion client, you might create personas representing the eco-conscious millennial, the style-focused Gen Z shopper, and the ethically driven family buyer. Each persona, when primed with the right data, can respond with realistic attitudes, preferences and language patterns.

Visual territories and creative exploration

While researching this book, I interviewed Morten Legarth, the Creative Director at Faith, an AI-first agency spun out of VCCP. He shared an important insight from their internal survey:

> 'Most people said AI has made them more creative. That's a hard thing for creatives to admit because creativity feels like it should come from within. But the fact that so many people say it has made them more creative is revealing. It hasn't necessarily made them more creative; it's just allowed them to more easily access their creativity.'

Imagine for a moment that, instead of exploring to two or three visual directions, you could explore ten creative territories for your sustainable fashion brand. Here's what you might explore:

- Earthy, natural aesthetics that emphasise the organic materials
- Clean, minimalist approaches that suggest premium quality
- Bold, colourful directions that challenge preconceptions about eco-fashion
- Documentary-style photography that tells supply chain stories
- Artistic, abstract representations of sustainability concepts

Using an LLM to explore ideas and an image generator to visualise them, a couple of people can explore each direction in the space of a day, and quickly get a feel for what's working. You can generate prototypes or mood boards showing how the brand might appear across different touchpoints – from packaging to retail environments to social media.

Once you've identified the strongest creative direction, AI helps bring those ideas to life in ways that sell the vision to your client. You can generate detailed storyboards for brand films, create mockups showing how the visual identity extends across different media, and even animate still images to demonstrate how static designs might work in motion. For our sustainable fashion brand, you might generate visualisations of pop-up shop concepts, show how the brand's sustainable story could unfold across a series of social media posts, or create previsualisations of advertising campaigns across different channels. For a campaign concept around 'clothes that last', you might generate images showing garments in various life stages, or create abstract visualisations of durability and craftsmanship.

AI allows you to test how different visual approaches might resonate before committing to expensive photoshoots or illustration commissions. This is where AI's ability to place concepts in context becomes invaluable. Instead of asking clients to imagine how abstract concepts might work in reality, instead you're actually showing them.

Content creation and scaling

With creative direction approved, AI becomes essential for content creation and scaling. This is where the technology proves its operational worth. You might start by developing comprehensive tone-of-voice guidelines using an AI analysis of your client's existing communications, preferred reference brands and strategic positioning. For our sustainable fashion brand, these guidelines might specify how to balance environmental messaging with style-focused content, how to communicate sustainability without preaching, and how to adapt tone across different audience segments and platforms.

Those guidelines then enable systematic content creation. Write one comprehensive piece about the brand's sustainability practices – perhaps a detailed blog post about supply chain transparency, for example – and AI can then repurpose this core content into:

- A series of social media posts, each highlighting a different aspect
- Email newsletter content for different customer segments
- Website copy explaining the brand's values
- Sales training materials for retail partners
- A press release for media outreach
- Presentation talking points for trade shows

Each adaptation maintains consistent messaging while being optimised for its specific context and audience.

Campaign development and execution

As your sustainable fashion campaign develops, AI supports increasingly sophisticated applications. You can generate custom soundtracks that match your brand film's emotional arc, create brand-specific voices for audio content, and develop campaign variations tailored to different markets or customer segments – just like Coca-Cola's 110 cityscapes in their Christmas ads.

The technology excels at campaign ideation, too. Input your core brand positioning and target audience insights, and AI can suggest campaign concepts, content series ideas and activation opportunities. For your sustainable fashion brand, this might generate ideas around clothing swap events, behind-the-scenes content series or partnerships with environmental organisations.

AI also transforms campaign performance analysis. Instead of manually correlating data across different channels, AI can identify patterns and relationships between marketing tactics, predict how different audience segments might respond to campaign elements, and suggest specific optimisations based on real-time performance data.

The operational backbone

Throughout this entire process, AI handles the operational tasks that typically eat into creative thinking time. Meeting transcriptions automatically become action-item lists and project updates. Feedback from multiple clients gets consolidated into clear themes and priorities. Project status reports write themselves based on your tracking systems. You can use AI to draft proposals for additional work, create case studies from completed projects, and handle routine documentation like terms and conditions or standard operating procedures. When your sustainable fashion client asks for a social media policy or influencer collaboration guidelines, a well-prompted AI can generate first drafts that your team then polish, generating detailed documentation in considerably less time.

What's remarkable about this comprehensive approach is how each AI application builds on the others. The research insights inform the strategy development. The strategic thinking guides the creative exploration. The creative concepts drive the content creation. The content creation supports the campaign execution. Each stage becomes more powerful because of what has come before. Your sustainable fashion brand campaign doesn't just look polished – it's strategically grounded, creatively rich and operationally efficient. You've been able to explore more creative territories, test more strategic approaches and develop more comprehensive content than would have been possible with traditional methods.

The agencies embracing this comprehensive approach aren't just working faster – they're delivering fundamentally better work. They spend less time on research drudgery and more time on strategic insight. Less time on operational tasks and more time on creative breakthrough. When AI handles the heavy lifting of research, analysis and content adaptation, human creativity can focus on what it does best: insight, strategy and breakthrough thinking that will give your clients a genuine competitive advantage.

Making it real for your clients

Hopefully, you are now starting to see that AI doesn't just make agencies more efficient, but also makes them more effective. Your clients get deeper strategic insights, more thoroughly explored creative territories, and more comprehensive campaign execution. They get better work, not just faster work. That's the fundamental shift agencies need to understand. AI isn't about doing the same things cheaper and quicker. It's about doing dramatically better things, more comprehensively, with greater strategic depth and creative exploration than was previously possible.

Great ideas there, but what tools should I use?

One of the first questions I get from agencies when we first start working with them is 'What's the best tool for... <insert activity>?'. Meanwhile, the CEO is worried that if they need twenty different AI tools to support their way of working, each with multiple licences across their teams, their technology budget is going to double.

Since the end of 2022, when generative AI first emerged into the public sphere, there has been a Cambrian explosion of AI tools. There are so many, with so many more launching every week, that it can be impossible to keep track even for people like me who are firmly in the AI bubble. To give you an idea of what I mean, the website There's an AI for That (or TAAFT for short) tracks most of the AI tools out there.[16] A screenshot I took in May 2024 shows 12,417 tools registered on the site, and now, in mid August 2025, it shows just under 40,000, suggesting there are on average over 2,000 new tools being released every month. Nobody can keep track of that, and to be honest, you shouldn't even bother.

Everything I have described above you can do with just three tools:

1. A meeting assistant (eg Fireflies, Otter or TL;DV)
2. An LLM (such as ChatGPT, Gemini or Claude)
3. An image generator (like Midjourney, or you can access a whole range through sites such as Krea and Freepik)

All the other tools you've heard of, and all the ones listed on sites like TAAFT, are built on top of just a handful of foundation models like ChatGPT or Stable Diffusion. They re-skin one of these existing models, and add an interface and custom instructions that make them suited to a particular task. They help you access the power of AI, but without the learning curve. As I said at the beginning of this chapter, AI is like some IKEA furniture, but without an instruction manual for what all the different bits actually do. These applications are trying to fix that for you, giving you clear ways of working and hiding the complexity behind a nice interface. That's great, but it gets expensive, fast.

However, with a little bit of skill, you don't need any of these. Armed with a language model, image generator and meeting assistant you can do pretty much anything you want. Sure, as time goes on, you may find there are specialist applications that perform certain tasks useful for your workflow such as Descript, a powerful podcast editor, or Waldo, a helpful research and briefing tool. Through Adobe, Google and Microsoft, you are likely to have access to some powerful features in the products you already use.

So stop procrastinating and just get started. Pick one tool in each of the categories above and start using them.

Should you use ChatGPT, Copilot or Gemini? It just doesn't matter – go with whichever one fits in best with your other platforms. They are all good, and they are all getting better all the time. One month one might be slightly ahead, and the next month something else is. Wait another month and your chosen tool is back on top. Screen out the noise, because the biggest differentiator in performance between any of these tools is you, and how you use them.

Key takeaways

- **Stop thinking of AI as just another production tool.** It's your creative partner from brief to delivery, transforming how you research, strategise, ideate and collaborate.

- **The real power lies in the beginning and middle stages.** While everyone focuses on final outputs, AI's biggest impact comes from enhancing research, strategy development and creative exploration.

- **You can access transformational capabilities for the price of a coffee.** ChatGPT, Midjourney and Claude offer world-class AI for less than £30 monthly, making technology access a non-issue.

- **Everything becomes explorable at speed.** Instead of choosing between two or three creative directions due to time constraints, you can now explore dozens and focus your energy on selecting and refining the best.

- **AI transforms the iceberg of invisible work.** Research that took days happens in hours, mood boards that required extensive sourcing can be generated in minutes, leaving more time for strategic thinking and creative refinement.

- **Quality comes from combination, not automation.** The best results blend AI's speed and breadth with human judgement, taste and strategic understanding.

- **Three tools cover 80% of your needs.** A meeting assistant, an LLM and an image generator handle most creative workflows without requiring dozens of specialist applications.

- **Your creative process becomes your competitive advantage.** Agencies that systematically integrate AI across their entire workflow will deliver fundamentally better work, not just faster work.

> **Your action point: Run a creative process audit**
>
> Take twenty minutes to map your last significant client project from brief to delivery. List every major activity (research, strategy, creative development, production, client management). For each activity, ask yourself, 'Could AI have enhanced this stage?' and 'What would we have explored differently with unlimited creative capacity?'
>
> Identify the three activities where AI could have had the biggest impact on either quality or exploration. These should become your priority areas for AI integration – the specific workflows where small changes could deliver disproportionate value for both your team and your clients.

5
How to speak AI

When we survey agencies before working with them, the same two barriers come up every time. First, they don't know what to use AI for (we've just sorted that in Chapter 4). Second, they can't get decent results out of the tools. Sure, AI can help draft an email, but how do you make it actually useful for real client work?

These tools can create pretty much anything. The hard part isn't getting them to work – it's getting them to create what you actually want. That's why WPP is throwing hundreds of millions at their AI platforms. They're running models on their own servers, training them on years of brand data – copy, images, campaigns, performance metrics – then building slick interfaces so users never see the complexity underneath. It's like having a creative team that's absorbed every brief, every campaign, every brand guideline you've ever produced.

However, here's what's remarkable about this moment: for once, technology isn't the barrier. You've got access to the same world-class models that WPP uses, for the price of a decent coffee each week. World-changing technology has never been this accessible. You just need to learn how to drive it.

These tools can generate full-length novels, feature films, entire advertising campaigns. The challenge isn't capability – it's control, and getting consistent tone of voice, an on-brand look and feel, and outputs that actually solve your specific problem. You need to control the chaos. Here, there are three techniques that work every time:

1. **Thinking** – Using your brain before and after you use AI
2. **Prompting** – Talking to AI like you'd brief your best intern
3. **Informing** – Giving AI the context it needs to be brilliant

Master these three, and you'll wonder how you ever worked without AI. Let's break them down.

1. Thinking: Don't switch off your brain

AI is brilliant at being average. Feed it a brief, and it'll serve up something polished and professional… and utterly predictable. It's the creative equivalent of a well-dressed person with nothing interesting to say. AI operates within the confines of its training data – everything that's already been done, said and published. Lean on it too heavily, and you risk getting trapped in an echo chamber of recycled ideas. Your unique perspective, honed by years of messy client meetings and creative breakthroughs, gets sidelined. That's a massive loss. AI doesn't dream. It doesn't understand your client's weird brand quirks or the brilliant insight that came to you in the shower this morning. It predicts patterns based on what's come before – it doesn't invent what's never been tried. It's at its best when it's amplifying your intelligence, not replacing it.

So here's how to stay in control:

- **Start with your own thinking.** Don't jump straight into ChatGPT the moment you get a brief. Sketch the idea first. Ask the hard questions. What's the story here? What angle is everyone else missing? Once you engage with AI tools, they'll naturally narrow your thinking and may drag you down paths you never intended. Have a clear sense of what good looks like before you even open your laptop.

- **Challenge the first answer.** AI loves serving up the obvious – the safe, expected response that ticks all the boxes but excites no one. Ask it again. Flip the brief. Add friction. Push it to explore uncomfortable territories. The breakthrough thinking is often hiding in the second, third or tenth response, not the first polished attempt.

- **Use it to explore, not decide.** Want ten design directions in ten minutes? Perfect. Need a list of headline options to spark your thinking? Brilliant. But you choose the winner. You edit the output. You own the final call. AI can show you possibilities, but your creative judgement determines which ones are worth pursuing.

- **Don't swallow everything whole.** AI speaks with the confident tone of an expert, but remember that it's only making educated guesses. Your experience and instincts are the final quality control. If something doesn't feel right, trust that feeling. You know what good work looks like for your clients better than any algorithm ever will.

- **Always fact-check.** These models still confuse details, mix up statistics, and occasionally invent 'facts' that sound convincing but which simply aren't true. Before making any important decisions based on AI-generated information, verify it against primary sources. Your reputation depends on accuracy, not speed.

- **Inject your voice.** AI can draft the bones, but it can't create resonance. Everything that comes out of these tools needs to run through your creative filter. Add your tone, your insight, your edge – the stuff that makes work memorable rather than just competent.

The most impactful creative work happening right now sits at the intersection of human intuition and machine speed. It's where creatives use AI to explore faster, go wider and dig deeper – but never disappear from the process. The algorithm can't predict your next brilliant idea or understand why breaking the rules might be exactly what your client needs.

Stay curious, stay engaged, and, most importantly, stay in the driver's seat. The tools are powerful, but the creative vision? That's still entirely yours.

2. Prompting: Your new creative language

Back in 2023, everyone was obsessed with 'prompt engineering' as the essential new skill. LinkedIn was buzzing with predictions that job boards would soon overflow with 'Prompt Engineer' roles. Agencies would be desperately headhunting these mystical prompt wizards who could somehow coax genius from ChatGPT with the perfect combination of words.

Here we are two years later. Where are they all?

The reality is both simpler and more complex than anyone predicted. Prompt engineers do exist – but they're not sitting in creative agencies crafting the perfect Instagram campaign brief. Real prompt engineers work deep in software development, building applications that call AI models thousands of times per day through APIs. They obsess over milliseconds of response time and fractions of pennies per query because their prompts are the invisible engine driving entire products. That's actual prompt engineering – technical, precise and largely invisible to the rest of us. Here's what the hype merchants missed: while you don't need to become a prompt engineer, mastering the art of prompting is absolutely crucial for creative professionals. It's not about learning some mystical incantation that unlocks AI's hidden powers. It's about developing a mindset that treats AI as your most versatile creative partner – one that can research like a junior strategist, ideate like a seasoned creative, and execute like a production team, all rolled into one incredibly patient collaborator.

Andrej Karpathy, one of the founders of OpenAI, captured this perfectly in early 2023 when he tweeted: 'The hottest new programming language is English'.[17] He's absolutely right, and here's why that should excite you rather than intimidate you. You already speak fluent English, so you've mastered half the skills you need. The other half? Learning to treat English somewhat like a programming language – structured, specific and purposeful. Think about how you brief a junior creative versus how you chat with a mate down the pub. The difference isn't just formality – it's clarity, context and intention. The same principle applies to AI, but with even greater rewards for getting it right.

Meet your new teammate: The brilliant paradox

When you first start working with AI, it feels uncannily like meeting a new colleague – but one who embodies a fascinating contradiction. Imagine someone who simultaneously has access to the sum of all human knowledge yet knows nothing about your specific business. Someone who can write in the style of Shakespeare, analyse market trends like a McKinsey consultant, and generate visual concepts like a seasoned art director, but needs you to explain in detail who your client is, what their brand actually stands for, where the client brief is stored on your computer, and what the structure of the strategy document you're trying to complete actually looks like.

This creates two distinct personalities you'll encounter. First, there's the brilliant graduate recruit. They're sharp, eager and overflowing with potential, but they're fresh out of university with zero experience in your particular world. Like any new hire, they need guidance, context and clear direction to channel their talents effectively. Second, there's the confident former boss who has an opinion about everything. They'll tackle any question you throw at them with the assured tone of someone who's seen it all before. They're brilliant at connecting dots and extrapolating insights – but what you're getting is an educated opinion dressed up as fact. Sometimes they're spot on. Sometimes they're confidently wrong.

Understanding this duality shapes how you should interact with AI. You're not consulting an all-knowing oracle that dispenses perfect answers. You're briefing a capable but inexperienced team member who needs your expertise to shine.

Consider the difference between these two approaches. You could ask: 'Come up with some interesting campaign ideas for our client'. That's like telling your new graduate hire to 'make something good happen' on their first day. You'll get a response, but it's likely to be generic, obvious or completely off-brand.

Or you could try: 'We're developing a campaign to target environmentally conscious millennials aged twenty-five to thirty for our client's new line of sustainable beachwear made from recycled ocean plastic. Our audience values style as much as sustainability – they won't compromise on looking good to feel good about their environmental impact. Research current trends in sustainable fashion marketing and suggest three campaign concepts that position our brand as the stylish choice for conscious consumers'.

The word 'prompting' is misleading because it makes the process sound quick and simple. When you interact with AI, you're essentially briefing a colleague. What's everything they need to know to have a good chance of completing the task well? This shift from thinking about 'prompts' to thinking about 'briefs' is fundamental to unlocking AI's potential in creative work.

The anatomy of a prompt

There are lots of prompt frameworks out there, but fundamentally they all recommend the same things. Give the model clear context, describe the task you want it to perform, guide it to the right answer and provide it with the data it needs. The one we use at Spark is the CICI framework (think 'cheeky' – now you'll remember it) – Character, Instructions, Criteria and Inputs. Consistently think of these four elements when you work with an LLM and you'll start to unlock their power.

Character: Set the stage. This is where most people fall short. They assume the AI knows their industry, understands their client's position in the market, or grasps the subtle brand nuances that inform every creative decision. AI doesn't know any of this unless you tell it. Start by defining the role you want the AI to play: 'You're a brand strategist specialising in sustainable fashion' will give you different insights to 'You're a social media manager for Gen Z audiences'. Then share the background information that would brief any human colleague: market position, target audience insights, brand personality, competitive landscape and the specific challenge you're trying to solve. The richer the context, the more relevant and useful the output.

Instructions: Be surgically precise. Vague requests generate vague responses. 'Help with our email marketing' will get you generic advice. 'Create a three-email sequence to launch our limited-edition summer collection, with the first email building anticipation, the second highlighting our unique sustainability story, and the third creating urgency around the limited quantities' gives the AI a clear target to aim for. Break down complex tasks into specific steps and be explicit about what you want the AI to focus on.

Criteria: Define the boundaries. AI won't magically guess your brand voice or preferred format. It might default to corporate-speak when you need conversational warmth, or produce an academic essay when you need snappy social media captions. Set clear parameters: 'Our brand voice is knowledgeable but never condescending, passionate about sustainability but never preachy, and always optimistic about positive change'. Define the format precisely: 'Present each email with a subject line, preview text, body copy divided into clear sections, and a specific call-to-action. Keep body copy under 150 words per email'. These constraints will ensure you get something you can actually use.

Inputs: Show what good looks like. AI is exceptionally good at pattern recognition. Feed it examples of work you admire – whether it's previous campaigns that performed well, competitor approaches you respect or reference points from completely different industries that capture the tone you're after. Upload client briefs, brand guidelines, successful case studies or tone-of-voice examples. Don't give it everything – it might get confused – but give it documents and data that are directly relevant to the task. These inputs calibrate the AI's understanding of what 'good' looks like in your specific context and dramatically improve the relevance of its output.

Think of this framework as directing a team rather than doing all the work yourself. Give brilliant people a brilliant brief using

Character, Instructions, Criteria and Inputs, and they'll consistently deliver brilliant work.

The prompt is just the beginning: The art of creative conversation

Here's what most people miss about AI: the first response is never the answer. It's the opening move in what should be a genuinely creative conversation. Yet I consistently watch professionals craft a prompt, hit enter, receive an answer and then stop. LLMs are not like Google, and stopping at the first answer it gives you wastes one of AI's most powerful capabilities – its ability to iterate, refine and explore ideas through dialogue.

Our best work rarely emerges fully formed. It develops through exploration, questioning, refinement and the kind of productive friction that comes from pushing ideas in unexpected directions. AI excels at this iterative process, but only if you treat it as a conversation partner rather than a vending machine. In our workshops, we often give teams a fictional client brief based on a sustainable fashion campaign. The initial AI-generated concepts are predictably safe – earnest messaging about saving the planet, obvious imagery of pristine beaches, conventional appeals to environmental guilt. Most people would either accept these mediocre ideas and lower their standards, or conclude that AI isn't capable of creative thinking.

But watch what happens when you start a real conversation: 'These concepts feel too predictable. Our audience already cares about the environment – they don't need convincing.

How might we approach this if our primary message is about style and confidence, with sustainability as the compelling backstory?' Suddenly, the AI explores fashion-forward directions that happen to be sustainable, rather than sustainable products trying to be fashionable. Push further: 'How could we bring these concepts to life as experiential marketing in pop-up stores?' Now you're getting ideas about sustainable fashion studios where customers can see ocean plastic being transformed into fabric, or interactive installations that visualise the environmental impact of different clothing choices. Each response opens new avenues for exploration. 'What assumptions are we making about our target audience that might be wrong?' helps stress-test your strategic thinking. 'How would a luxury brand approach this same challenge?' introduces different reference points. 'What would this look like if we had half the budget but twice the creativity?' forces innovative solutions.

I've watched a copywriter develop complete tone-of-voice guidelines through this iterative process. She started with a basic brief for a brand voice and received competent but generic initial guidelines. Instead of settling, she engaged in dialogue: 'The conversational approach works well, but the humour feels too sarcastic for our brand. How can we maintain wit while feeling more supportive?' Each refinement brought the output closer to her vision. By the fifth exchange, the tone-of-voice examples were so precisely aligned that her creative director assumed she'd written them herself. What's fascinating is that she couldn't have articulated exactly what she wanted at the beginning. The conversation itself clarified her thinking, helping her discover nuances she hadn't consciously recognised. This is AI at its most powerful – amplifying your ideas through structured exploration.

This conversational approach transforms AI from a simple query-response tool into a dynamic thought partner. Unlike human colleagues, your AI collaborator has perfect recall of everything you've discussed, infinite patience for exploration and no ego investment in particular ideas. You can ask it to argue against its own suggestions, explore contradictory approaches or dive deep into tangential ideas without worrying about time constraints or hurt feelings.

One workshop participant described it perfectly:

> 'It's like having access to a whole creative department, all working on different aspects of the same challenge. I can ask the researcher for insights, then the strategist for positioning options, then the copywriter for execution ideas, then the critic to tear it all apart – all within the same conversation.'

This dialogue-driven approach also helps overcome AI's inherent limitations. No single prompt, however detailed, can anticipate every nuance of your creative challenge. But through conversation, you can navigate around gaps in understanding, inject your specific expertise and guide the AI toward increasingly valuable responses. The magic isn't in finding the perfect prompt – it's in developing the skill to have genuinely productive creative conversations with AI.

The professionals who embrace this conversational mindset consistently report breakthrough insights and unexpected creative directions. Those who treat AI as a one-shot answer machine remain disappointed by generic outputs. The difference isn't in the technology – it's in the approach.

An example of a poor prompt and a good prompt

Bad Prompt:

> Write a shot list for a new fashion shoot

Good prompt:

> **Character:**
>
> You are a seasoned fashion photographer and creative director working on a high-end fashion shoot. The focus of the shoot is to showcase the brand's latest collection, emphasising elegance, versatility and accessibility. The images will be used across digital, print and in-store marketing.
>
> **Instructions:**
>
> Develop a detailed shot list that captures the essence of our brand identity. Include a mix of hero shots, lifestyle imagery, close-ups and candid moments. Ensure the visuals appeal to the target audience (stylish, quality-conscious consumers). Consider settings, poses, lighting and styling directions. Specify any special elements such as movement, interaction or emotion to be conveyed. Keep in mind social media formats, catalogue layouts and billboard crops.
>
> **Criteria:**
>
> *Tone*: timeless, sophisticated, yet approachable

Location: studio and on-location (urban and nature-inspired)

Wardrobe focus: seasonal highlights (eg layering for autumn, breezy fabrics for summer)

Lighting preferences: soft natural light for lifestyle shots, studio lighting for editorial impact

Must-haves:

- Hero shots of key outfits
- Detail shots of fabrics, textures and accessories
- Group shots showing effortless styling
- Motion shots (eg walking, adjusting clothing naturally)
- Interaction shots (eg friends, family, real-life scenarios)
- Seasonal mood shots (rainy day layering, summer in the city, cosy indoors)

Inputs:

Collection details: (Insert collection brief)

Target audience insights: (Insert audience profile)

Campaign concept: (Insert creative direction)

Building a library of prompts

As you work with these tools, you'll start to see patterns in what works best. That's the time to start saving your prompts. Think of them as recipes – tested, refined and ready to produce consistent results. Over time, this library will become an invaluable resource for recurring tasks, from drafting proposals to summarising reports.

3. Informing: Everything is now data

When you read a client brief, you bring years of experience and domain knowledge to its interpretation. You understand the industry jargon, you can read between the lines about what the client really wants, and you know the unstated constraints of the market.

I've watched countless creative professionals fall into the same trap when working with AI tools. They assume the AI can somehow intuit the unspoken context or fill in the blanks with industry knowledge. It can't. Your AI assistant is brilliantly capable but ultimately limited by the information you provide. Without explicit context, it's like asking a talented new hire to develop a strategy without giving them the client brief.

Think of it like this: AI doesn't have access to the mental library you've built throughout your career. That library – filled with case studies, competitor insights and cultural references – is what allows you to transform a vague brief into brilliant work. To unlock the true potential of AI, you need to share that library.

Consider how you approach your creative work. When crafting a brand strategy or designing a campaign, what information do you draw upon? The brief, certainly, but also additional details the client gave you on the kick-off call. The email thread where they clarified their objectives. Your team's brainstorming session. The competitor analysis your colleague briefed you on this morning. The brand guidelines. A similar project you worked on last year. That article you read in *Marketing Week* last month. Perhaps even your own handwritten notes from the train journey to work.

This amalgamation of formal and informal inputs is your context. It's the rich soil from which your creative ideas grow. Now, all of it can be data for your AI assistant.

In one workshop, a strategist from a London agency demonstrated this approach brilliantly. She was developing positioning options for a boutique hotel chain and began by uploading the formal client brief. However, then she went further, adding the recorded client interview, customer review analysis, photographs of competitor properties and even some rough sketches from her initial ideation session. The difference in quality between her first prompt (using just the brief) and her contextually rich approach was stark. 'It's like the AI went from being a generic consultant to actually understanding our specific challenge,' she explained.

I've found that the agencies getting the most value from AI are those treating it as a team member who needs comprehensive onboarding to a project. They wouldn't expect a new strategist to deliver insightful work without access to all relevant materials, and they apply the same principle to their AI tools.

Here are some ideas of what to feed into your AI tools:

- Client briefs and documentation. The formal requirements and background.
- Meeting transcripts. Use that notetaker; there's a richness of information and nuance in conversation that you can't get anywhere else.

- Email threads. The clarifications and evolving understanding.

- Research materials. Market insights and data that inform decisions.

- Team brainstorms. The collaborative thinking that sparked ideas.

- Brand guidelines. The established parameters and visual language.

- Previous campaign materials. The historical context and what's worked before.

- Your handwritten notes. Yes, even those scribbles can be photographed and used.

Don't overdo it. Just like you don't want to overwhelm the intern with information that, while interesting, isn't directly relevant to the task at hand, *treat your AI assistant* the same way. Make your data relevant and watch your outputs transform.

A senior copywriter I trained last autumn described this approach as 'giving the AI access to my brain'. She now routinely uploads her personal research notes, voice memos from client meetings, and even relevant articles she's saved to her reading list. 'The quality of what I get back is directly proportional to the richness of what I put in,' she notes. 'It's the difference between getting generic category writing and something that genuinely feels informed by our specific project context.'

Remember, AI doesn't have inherent knowledge of your client, their market or your agency's approach. However, when you provide that context, you transform a powerful but generic tool into something that feels almost like a custom extension of your own creative thinking – a partner that understands not just the explicit brief, but all the subtleties that make your work distinctive and valuable.

Creating custom AI assistants

Now you know how to craft brilliant briefs, talk to AI like a valued colleague, and feed it exactly the right information to get exceptional results. Here's the exciting part: imagine you could make that perfectly briefed colleague available to everyone on your team.

OpenAI calls them custom GPTs, Gemini calls them Gems, and Copilot calls them Agents. Whatever the name, these pre-trained assistants represent one of the most practical ways to AI-enable your entire workflow.

Imagine your agency works with clients ranging from luxury fashion brands to fintech startups. Each client has wildly different tone requirements, brand guidelines and creative expectations. A generic AI model might give you competent but generic results across these diverse needs, but custom AI assistants can truly excel for specific clients or tasks. Think of custom AI assistants as specialist team members rather than generalists. Just as you might have copywriters who instinctively understand the language of luxury brands, or designers with a particular flair for tech startup aesthetics, you can now create AI specialists tailored to distinct clients, sectors or creative challenges. The beauty is that, once you've built these specialists, anyone on your team can access that expertise instantly. Your junior account manager can tap into the same brand-specific knowledge that took your senior strategist years to develop. Your freelance designer can immediately understand a client's visual preferences without lengthy briefing sessions. It's like having your best people available 24/7, ready to share their expertise with anyone who needs it.

By developing these specialist assistants for your key clients or common tasks, you're not automating work (you will usually need to manually tweak and refine the outputs, in any case); instead, you're creating intelligent extensions of your agency's unique approach and understanding.

Here's how you can set up these custom specialists for your own agency.

1. Define the scope with precision

Begin by identifying exactly what you need this custom assistant to do. At the core of a custom GPT, Copilot Agent or Gemini Gem is a prompt. The clearer and more focused the prompt is, the more effective your assistant will be.

Examples might be:

- Turning client meeting notes into follow up emails
- Drafting client-specific LinkedIn posts
- Generating digital campaign concepts
- Brainstorming event activations
- Producing tailored content for pitch decks following your agency's framework
- Converting case studies into awards entries

Document these goals to create a clear focus. For instance, a luxury fashion client may require a tone of understated elegance with specific terminology and references, while a fintech startup might need approachable explanations of complex concepts with a confident, forward-thinking edge.

2. Gather rich, representative data

This is where many agencies fall short – they provide insufficient examples for the assistant to truly understand your distinctive approach, rendering the results too generic and a bit... *meh*.

One content agency I trained showed me the dramatic difference in their results after they expanded their training data. Initially, they'd only included the client's brand guidelines. When they added successful past campaigns, transcripts from client feedback sessions and competitor analyses, their custom assistant began producing work that captured not just the surface-level tone but the deeper strategic patterns that made their client's communications successful.

Compile examples such as:

- Creative briefs and campaign outlines
- Brand guidelines and tone-of-voice documents
- Sample ads, press releases and social media posts
- Client feedback on past work (both positive and negative)
- Competitive analyses highlighting positioning differences

This rich context becomes the foundation for your assistant's understanding. For instance, if a client consistently prefers concise, impactful language with a specific structure to their communications, these patterns will be embedded into the assistant's responses.

3. Craft your training prompt with care

The instructions you provide when creating your custom assistant are crucial – they're effectively your ongoing brief to this new team member. Your prompt should include everything we've covered earlier:

- A clear explanation of its role
- Detailed instructions about how to approach its task
- Context about the documents you have provided it (eg the transcript from a client call or the notes from a brainstorming session) and how to use them to guide the task
- Examples of what a good answer looks like
- Common pitfalls or inconsistencies to avoid
- The structure of the output you would like it to create

Remember, you don't need technical expertise here – you need creative and strategic clarity about what you are trying to achieve.

4. Test rigorously and iterate thoughtfully

Once your custom assistant is set up, like any new hire, it needs feedback and refinement. Test your assistant on real-world tasks:

- Does it produce copy that captures the required tone?
- Are its ideas aligned with your client's strategic direction?
- Does it avoid the typical clichés of the category?
- Can it adapt to different contexts while maintaining brand consistency?

Dive back into the instructions or add additional data until it is giving you consistent, useful responses. Remember, don't try and make its task too broad; custom assistants perform best when used for a specific thing – proposal drafting or ideating from a creative brief.

A digital marketing team I advised created a systematic testing process for their custom GPT. They ran it through a series of standard briefs, comparing its output with work their senior creatives had produced for similar requests. They identified specific patterns where the assistant excelled or fell short, then refined its instructions accordingly.

AI assistants in action

Custom AI assistants aren't just theoretical tools – they're becoming integral parts of creative teams across our industry. When thoughtfully integrated into your agency's workflow, these assistants can transform how you brainstorm, draft, refine and collaborate. I've watched our AI Accelerator clients evolve from cautiously experimenting to confidently integrating AI assistants as they discover the practical power of these tools in their day-to-day work.

AI assistants truly shine when embedded into collaborative processes. They don't replace your team but they can extend its capabilities, much like how a photography assistant allows the photographer to focus on creative direction rather than technical setup. Picture how this might transform typical agency workflows:

Brainstorming sessions

During an initial campaign meeting for a wellness brand, a team prompts their custom assistant to generate concept territories aligned with the client's emphasis on accessible mindfulness. The assistant, trained on the brand's previous campaigns and audience research, suggests 'everyday calm' as a concept – exploring how small, mindful moments could fit into busy lives. This direction resonated with the team, who then build upon it with their own insights and expertise, creating a campaign that the client immediately connected with.

Briefing and critiquing

A copywriting agency have created a fully AI-augmented workflow, but crucially, all the copy is still being written by humans. AI assistants interrogate the client brief and automatically send back questions to clarify anything that isn't clear. Then a research assistant gathers all the background information required for the piece. The human copywriter can then set to work with everything they need to get started. Once they're done, another AI assistant provides the first round of feedback, assessing the copy against the client's brief and tone-of-voice guidelines and suggesting improvements. By the time the copy hits the client's inbox, they get a 90% first-time acceptance rate.

Not only that, their writers love it because they get to do what they do best – write copy – while all the boring stuff – going back and forwards on the brief, handling client revisions – is largely handled for them.

Visualisation acceleration

A creative studio has integrated a custom assistant into the gap between brand positioning and design. Their assistant, trained on successful past campaigns, transforms written concepts into detailed image prompts for Midjourney and Adobe Firefly. It converted a campaign concept about 'urban nature reconnection' into specific visual prompts like 'urban professional in linen clothing walking through dappled sunlight in a city park, shot from low angle with morning light, cinematic, hopeful atmosphere'. These precisely crafted prompts give their designers a clear starting point, dramatically accelerating the visualisation process.

Client feedback integration

Perhaps one of the most valuable applications I've seen is in client management. An account director at a London agency feeds all client feedback emails and meeting transcripts into their custom assistant, which distils them into clear, actionable revisions. 'It catches nuances in client feedback that we sometimes miss in the moment,' she explained. 'Instead of generic notes like "client wants it more vibrant", we get specific direction like "increase colour saturation in lifestyle imagery while maintaining neutral tones for product shots, per client preference from previous campaign".'

Ten ideas for AI assistants

Want to see AI in action where it really counts? These examples show how leading strategists are building their own GPTs to solve everyday creative and strategic challenges – using their own data. Each one is a blueprint you can copy, tweak and deploy right now.

1. Audience persona GPT

Train a GPT on your client's segmentation data, user research and interview transcripts. Now, instead of guessing what your customer might say, you can ask. Roleplay with your target persona. Test positioning statements, campaign hooks and creative directions in a private, AI-powered chat: 'How would a twenty-eight-year-old urban parent respond to this slogan?' You get fast, realistic feedback without setting up a research sprint.

2. Brand-guideline GPT

Upload brand guidelines, tone-of-voice docs and past creative examples into one place. Then ask: 'Is this headline in line with our tone?' or 'Can I use this voice on TikTok as well as email?' No more flipping through style guides – your team gets brand-consistent decisions in seconds.

3. Competitive-intel GPT

Feed it competitor audits, market reports and brand analysis. Then ask: 'What positioning is Brand X using right now?' or 'What's the common thread across these three rival campaigns?' Because it's trained only on curated docs – not the open web – you get sharp, brand-relevant insights without the noise.

4. Workshop-planning GPT
If you run strategy or brand workshops, this is your digital facilitator. Load in your favourite techniques, icebreakers, feedback forms and templates. Then ask: 'What's a good warm-up for a cautious B2B team?' or 'Give me three exercises to get to a positioning statement'. It'll even suggest how to adapt content for different client personalities or objectives.

5. Creative brief GPT
Upload briefing templates, brand background and consumer insights. Then prompt it with something like: 'Generate a tight creative brief for our plant-based meat campaign', or 'Refine this sustainability message for a Gen Z audience'. The result? Briefs that are clear, consistent and always aligned with the strategy.

6. Customer-journey GPT
Map out the brand's sales funnel, friction points and personas. Then ask: 'What objections does a first-time buyer have?' or 'Where do people fall out of our sign-up flow?' Strategists can surface invisible gaps in the funnel and find ways to fix them.

7. Client opportunity identifier GPT
Upload your client's recent campaign data, industry news and your agency's case study library to spot untapped opportunities within an existing account. Then ask: 'What seasonal opportunities are we missing for this client?' or 'Which audience segments are underperforming

and why?' It identifies gaps your clients might not have recognised and crafts conversation starters with specific, data-backed insights that transform your client services team from order-takers to strategic partners.

8. Synthetic market research GPT
For concept testing or focus group simulations, feed the GPT real interview transcripts and broader research. Then prompt it to reply as: 'A budget-conscious single mum from Leeds', or 'A Gen Z flexitarian who shops on TikTok'. Not a full replacement for research – but a brilliant way to spot blind spots or pressure-test creative ideas before client review.

9. Manifesto and story GPT
Need to write a brand manifesto or origin story? Upload brand pillars, 'why' statements and creative references. Ask for: 'A short emotional script that captures our purpose', or 'A compelling story arc for a pitch deck'. The first draft's done – your team just shapes it with real-world texture.

10. Pitch and presentation GPT
Give it past pitch decks, visual references and successful case studies. Then ask: 'Create a narrative arc for our next pitch', or 'Tailor this deck for a health-tech audience'. You'll get consistent structure, reusable story flows and faster turnarounds for every new client or vertical.

Each one of these AI assistants starts with the same simple steps: upload the right documents, define a clear purpose and prompt it like a strategist – not a robot. Want to make it even easier? Create a shared folder of your most-used docs (briefs, decks, guidelines, templates) and build GPTs around each one. It's not about replacing your creative process; it's about accelerating it without losing your edge.

Key takeaways

- **Prompting isn't mystical engineering, it's a structured briefing.** Treat AI like your most capable intern who needs clear context, specific instructions, defined constraints and relevant examples to excel.

- **Three core skills unlock AI's potential.** Thinking strategically before and after using AI, prompting with structured briefs and informing tools with rich contextual data.

- **Conversation beats calculation.** The most powerful AI interactions feel like collaborative creative sessions with a tireless partner who has perfect recall and infinite patience.

- **The first response is never the best answer.** AI's real power emerges through iterative conversation, pushing back, refining ideas and exploring alternatives rather than accepting initial outputs.

- **Your brain stays in the driver's seat.** AI excels at being average and predictable, so start with your own thinking, challenge obvious responses and inject your unique perspective into everything.

- **Context is everything in the AI era.** Your meeting transcripts, email threads, brand guidelines and project notes become powerful training data that transforms generic tools into informed collaborators.

- **Custom AI assistants scale your expertise.** Building specialist GPTs, Gems or Agents that are trained on your specific processes and client knowledge makes your best thinking available to everyone on your team.

- **Data organisation directly impacts AI performance.** The 'intern test' applies perfectly: if a bright new hire couldn't quickly understand your projects and clients, neither can your AI tools.

> **Your action point: Build your first custom AI assistant**
>
> Spend an hour creating a custom GPT, Gemini Gem or Copilot Agent for one specific, recurring task in your agency (like 'Client Brief Analyser' or 'Campaign Concept Generator'). Upload three to five relevant documents as training data and write clear instructions about the assistant's role and approach. Test it with a real example from recent work, then refine the instructions based on the output quality. This hands-on exercise will teach you more about AI's capabilities and limitations than hours of reading, while creating a practical tool your team can use immediately.

6
Working with image generators

We've all seen the amusing side of generative AI – videos of Will Smith eating spaghetti or those uncanny images of people with hands resembling cauliflowers. That was so 2023. By 2025, this fast-evolving technology has become remarkably credible. While they haven't yet replaced traditional illustration, photography or film, they're certainly closing the gap and excelling as powerful creative accelerators.

Imagine you're in a client meeting and everything's going brilliantly. They love the strategy, they're nodding along with the positioning, they're excited about the campaign direction. Then you get to the visual concept. You describe it passionately – the mood, the aesthetic, the emotional impact. You can see it in their eyes: they just can't visualise what you're talking about. Sound familiar? We've all felt that frustrating gap between the brilliant visual idea locked inside our heads and getting it down onto screen or paper. Hours spent sketching roughs, teams trawling through endless stock photo libraries, trying desperately to capture that exact mood, that specific vibe. How much creative energy gets burned just trying to get everyone onto the same visual page? What if you could snap your fingers and conjure a visual interpretation of exactly that concept? Not rough sketches, but compelling, high-fidelity images, right there on screen, in minutes? That's exactly what AI image generators now make possible, and they're rapidly becoming essential creative accelerators that no agency can afford to ignore.

Why this changes everything

AI image generators turn text prompts into visuals – think of it like having an incredibly fast, remarkably versatile and utterly tireless junior designer who perfectly understands your concept. You brief them with words and they deliver the images you need. This goes to the heart of what agencies deliver to clients, directly impacting creativity, efficiency and client satisfaction. Remember those projects that got bogged down in endless mood board iterations? Or internal debates trying to align everyone on visual direction? These tools obliterate those bottlenecks, letting you generate concepts, explore styles and produce variations at speed. Need ten different takes on a campaign visual by lunchtime? No problem. But speed is just the beginning – the real power lies in visualising the unseen. One creative director captured this perfectly: 'One of the most frustrating things about group brainstorms is that you can't see what's in someone else's head. Now, we can visualise any idea and judge it on its own merit.' Instead of describing abstract concepts in client meetings, you show them. This accelerates decisions, quickly gets clients excited and reduces misalignment risk down the line. Most importantly, these tools fuel creative exploration beyond just doing the same things faster – they give you the bandwidth to explore more creative territory, test wilder ideas, blend unexpected styles and push boundaries without committing huge amounts of time or budget upfront.

Choosing your creative weapons

The landscape of AI image generators can feel overwhelming, but understanding which tool excels at what will save you time and frustration. Think of each as a specialist team member rather than a generalist. Just as you might have copywriters who excel at particular tones or designers with specific aesthetic strengths, these AI tools have distinct personalities and capabilities. There are lots of them out there. Here are a handful of the best.

Midjourney

Midjourney is renowned for producing high-quality, strikingly artistic outputs with beautiful unpredictability. This tool really understands complex stylistic requests and offers detailed control through dozens of parameters. Midjourney is great when you need illustration work – concept art, character design, imaginative storyboards – or photorealistic imagery that might be prohibitively expensive to stage in reality. Think fantastical scenes, historical reimaginings or that hyper-realistic photograph of Isaac Newton discovering gravity in bustling modern-day Tokyo for a quirky campaign. You can train it on your brand visuals to create consistent characters and objects across multiple generations. However it still struggles with accurate text rendering, so if your visual needs legible type you'll be heading back to Photoshop.

Ideogram

Ideogram gained attention as the text champion. Its latest model, v3, handles text rendering within images reasonably well, making it ideal for graphic design tasks where typography is integral. Choose Ideogram when you need to generate initial logo concepts, create eye-catching poster designs with headlines, or mock up social media graphics where the message needs visual embedding. Its Canvas feature lets you build mood boards and add text without leaving the app, while the batch upload feature allows you to generate up to 1,000 prompts automatically. Need to rapidly mock up ten different packaging concepts for a client presentation? Ideogram is an excellent starting point.

Flux and Stable Diffusion

Flux and Stable Diffusion are powerful open-source options offering significantly more control than others, with the trade-off of much greater complexity. WPP became an investor in Stable Diffusion in March 2025, and film director James Cameron sits on their board, a sign of serious industry interest.[18] Being open source, they can run locally on powerful machines, giving full control over data privacy. The most common front end is ComfyUI, allowing visual workflows that link nodes together to create virtually anything. It requires technical aptitude – anyone comfortable with coding website front-ends or writing Photoshop scripts would manage fine. Most importantly, it can be trained to generate consistent brand imagery from relatively small datasets. For agencies serious about integrating AI image generation into production workflows, this is the way to go.

Freepik and Krea

For agencies wanting simplicity over specialisation, platforms like Freepik.ai and Krea.ai combine multiple image- and video-generation engines under one subscription. For non-power users, this might be all you need without the complexity of managing multiple platforms.

Weavy and Flora

Anyone using these generators for real client work knows the current reality: you're constantly switching between ChatGPT for prompts, Midjourney for images, Runway for video, Photoshop for refinements and Premiere for video editing. Jumping between tools slows you down and gets exhausting fast. Flora and Weavy, both launched in early 2025, address exactly this problem, emphasising repeatable workflows across all these tools. With a node-based interface similar to ComfyUI but less complex, it allows teams to collaborate and connect text models with image models with video models seamlessly. Want to generate a multi-panel mood board, grab each frame, create image prompts, generate multiple colour versions, then animate everything ready for Premiere? Flora and Weavy can handle that entire workflow. These tools are definitely one to watch as the industry moves toward integrated creative workflows.[19]

Mastering the art of AI direction

Here's where most people go wrong with image generators: they treat them like language models. Type in a few keywords, hope for magic. However, these tools work on diffusion modelling – they're one-shot systems with no memory. You can't say 'yes, but make the car red' like you would with ChatGPT. If you don't like what you got, you start over with a completely new prompt. This creates a fundamental challenge: if you only use a handful of words to describe your image, you leave countless details unsaid. Anything you don't specify – time of day, colour, lighting, composition – the generator will imagine for you, and its imagination probably differs from yours. When you're ideating, that unpredictability can be brilliant. When you're trying to create something specific, it's frustrating chaos. The solution? Develop detailed prompts using a consistent framework. Think of it like writing a concise creative brief for the AI. For any image, consider these essential elements.

The basics

- **Medium:** What kind of picture is it? An iPhone photograph? A pencil sketch? A vector illustration? A 3D render? An advertising pack shot? A minimalist line drawing?

- **Created by:** A spray can of paint? A high-resolution digital camera? Coloured crayons? An old polaroid camera? For photographs, specifying the camera and lens can help.

- **Subject:** What is the main focus of the image? Be specific (eg 'a middle-aged Caucasian man with receding brown hair and olive skin wearing a pale green t-shirt' instead of just 'a man').

- **Action:** What is the subject doing? Where is it happening? (eg 'parked on a cliff overlooking a calm ocean at sunset' instead of 'outside').

- **Environment:** What are the surroundings? Plain white background? Clean modern kitchen with white worktops and large windows? A grid of graph paper with thin blue lines.

The craft

- **Camera angle:** From what angle are we seeing the subject? Eye level, low angle, overhead? Is this a telephoto shot or a super wide angle? Can we see all of the subject or is it a portrait just showing a person's head and shoulders?

- **Composition:** Is the subject centred or off on the left or right? What is in the foreground or background?

- **Lighting and time of day:** Is this in soft studio lighting or outdoors at dusk, or illuminated by streetlights through a window?

The feel

- **Period:** What time period and mood are you after? Contemporary, retro 1980s, futuristic and sleek?

- **Feeling:** What emotion are you trying to convey? Hopeful, sinister, optimistic, tense etc.

This structured approach transforms your relationship with AI image generation. Instead of randomly rolling dice, you're directing the output. Once you craft a structured prompt that gets close to what you want, you can iterate with surgical precision – change just one component while everything else stays consistent. Want that futuristic motorbike scene as a gritty graphic novel panel instead of a photo? Just change the medium component. Love the graphic novel style but want a classic cafe racer bike instead? Just change the subject. This iterative process gives you genuine control and makes AI feel like a tool you're wielding purposefully rather than hoping for lucky accidents.

Taking control with visual references

Text prompts are powerful, but adding image references gives you even greater control. Most serious image generation tools let you upload existing images to guide output alongside your words. This opens up game-changing possibilities.

Use **style references** when you've found an image with exactly the aesthetic, lighting or colour palette you're after. Upload it as a guide rather than struggling to describe 'that specific type of golden-hour lighting with soft shadows'.

Composition references work brilliantly for layouts and framing. Stop describing camera angles – show the AI what you want by uploading a reference image or even sketching a rough layout and photographing it.

Character and object references become crucial when you need consistency across multiple images – essential for campaigns or storytelling. Upload a reference image to maintain visual continuity as you generate different scenes with the same character or product.

This combination of structured text prompts and visual references moves you far from random chance toward predictable, directable creative output. You're giving the AI the clearest possible brief using both words and pictures.

Beyond still images: The moving picture

While image generators capture most attention, AI video and 3D tools are rapidly catching up, with possibilities that seemed impossible just months ago. Google's VEO 3, released in May 2025 alongside their AI editing suite, Flow, represents a massive leap forward in AI video generation. Unlike earlier tools that produced short, dreamlike clips with obvious AI tells, VEO 3 generates remarkably realistic footage up to several minutes long, complete with realistic audio. Describe 'a confident woman walking through a bustling London market at golden hour, shot on 35 mm film' and get back footage that looks professionally shot. Meanwhile, tools like Vizcom transform product visualisation workflows. Upload a rough product sketch and get back competent 3D renderings you can rotate, scale and contextualise. This proves particularly powerful for packaging design, product launches and client presentations where you need to show how concepts might look in reality.

The real-world revolution

The agencies already embracing these tools aren't just working faster – they're working fundamentally differently. One London creative director described the transformation:

> 'We used to spend weeks aligning on visual direction. Now we generate ten concepts in a couple of days, pick the strongest, and spend our time refining strategy and building client relationships instead of hunting through stock libraries.'

These tools still work best when combined with traditional workflows. AI generates initial concepts and variations quickly, then human designers refine and perfect the outputs that show most promise. A video generator creates some clips, but you still edit them in Premiere, DaVinci or Final Cut. It's acceleration, letting creative teams explore far more territory than traditional methods allow. I'd argue they're mostly not quite ready for final production except for low-res social ads, although Spark has created a brand film for a dairy company composed of a mixture of real and AI-generated clips which the client loved.

Your creatives remain essential for their vision, taste and strategic understanding. AI doesn't possess these qualities. The outputs need critical human curation, ruthless selection and almost always manual refinement using traditional tools like Photoshop or Illustrator. Don't expect print-ready perfection straight from AI – expect compelling raw potential that needs professional shaping.

The cumulative impact extends far beyond final artwork. Teams use AI image generation for detailed storyboards, spatial designs for events, unique presentation visuals that break free from template tedium, app graphics and icons, and concept exploration for website UI elements. The hours saved on image sourcing, initial sketching and graphic variations add up quickly, freeing valuable creative talent to focus on strategic thinking, client relationships and the truly unique aspects of each campaign. Most importantly, these tools transform client conversations. *Showing* remains more powerful than *telling*. Presenting compelling AI-generated visuals early in the process gets client buy-in faster, makes abstract concepts tangible and generates genuine excitement for creative direction. When you can visualise any idea instantly, brainstorms become more productive and decisions happen faster.

The agencies mastering this approach gain a genuine competitive advantage. They explore more creative territories, present more compelling pitches and deliver more thoroughly considered campaigns than traditional methods allow. This isn't about cutting costs – it's about raising creative standards.

Key takeaways

- **AI image generators are creative accelerators, not replacements.** They transform the frustrating gap between brilliant ideas in your head and getting clients to visualise them, enabling instant concept exploration.

- **Client conversations transform when ideas become visible.** Showing compelling AI-generated concepts early in the process accelerates decision making and generates genuine excitement for creative directions.

- **Structured prompting gives you creative control.** Detailed briefs covering subject, action, environment, lighting and style transform random outputs into directed creative exploration.

- **Visual references unlock precision.** Combining structured text prompts with uploaded reference images moves you from hoping for lucky accidents to systematically achieving your creative vision.

- **One-shot generation requires comprehensive thinking.** Unlike ChatGPT's conversational memory, image generators start fresh each time, making thorough initial prompts essential for consistent results.

- **The technology is rapidly approaching production quality.** While still requiring human refinement, AI-generated visuals are becoming sophisticated enough for professional creative work.

- **Integration matters more than individual tools.** Platforms like ComfyUI, Weavy and Flora that connect text, image and video generation into seamless workflows represent the future of AI-assisted creativity.

Your action point: Master the structured prompt framework

Pick a current creative brief and spend twenty minutes generating the same concept using both approaches: first, create an image using just a few keywords (your current instinct), then create another using the full structured framework from the chapter – medium, subject, action, environment, camera angle, lighting and mood.

Compare the results and note the difference in both quality and creative control. Then generate three variations of the structured prompt by changing only one element each time (eg lighting, camera angle or mood). This exercise will give you an intuitive understanding of how detailed direction transforms AI from a random generator into a precise creative tool.

Seriously, *do this*. Don't just think about it. The practical insights gained from even a short, focused experiment are worth far more than hours of reading articles. Go on, give it a try. You might just surprise yourself.

7
Data privacy, IP and ethics

When I run workshops on AI tools, there's always a moment when someone raises their hand with a concerned look and asks about the legal implications. They're right to ask. As creative professionals, we have obligations to our profession, our clients and the wider world when it comes to data privacy and intellectual property.

I should caveat everything here by saying that I am not a lawyer, but I am reasonably well read in this area and have spoken to two IP lawyers who specialise in this. Let's tackle this head-on with practical advice rather than legal jargon.

Is this stuff legal?

Let's talk about the elephant in the creative studio: almost every AI model you're using today has been trained on mountains of copyrighted material – without asking for permission. From the novels that helped ChatGPT understand narrative structure to the meticulously crafted illustrations that taught Midjourney about composition and style, creators' work has been swept up into these systems without their consent or compensation.

This isn't some theoretical concern – it's the foundation these tools are built upon. I've seen people tie themselves in knots justifying their AI adoption while avoiding this uncomfortable truth. At our workshops, this topic sparks some of the most passionate debates, with some refusing to touch LLMs and image generators out of solidarity with fellow artists, while others argue it's no different to how photography disrupted painting or how sampling transformed music. Some argue it is no different to how human brains gather and assimilate information over our lives to provide us with inspiration and remixes. To some degree, this is of course true, but AI models industrialise this process at vast scale, and do not compensate the rights holders. When you last got inspired by an author, artist or a musician, you had at least usually paid to read, see or hear their work.

There's no moral high ground here that I can offer you – only the challenge to make a decision that aligns with your values. Are you comfortable building your creative practice on tools trained this way? Will you limit your usage to certain applications? How will you explain your position to clients who ask? These aren't questions to delegate to your legal team – they go to the heart of your creative identity in the AI age. Whatever path you choose, I'd suggest one non-negotiable: be honest with yourself, your team and your clients about the ethical complexity underneath these seemingly magical creative assistants.

By reading this book, I'm assuming you have got past this point and are happy to use these tools for your work. If that's the case, then read this next section carefully.

The free tier trap

The number one rule for using AI tools professionally is simple: stop using free personal accounts for client work. In Silicon Valley, there's a saying: 'If the product is free, you are the product'. This is how Google and Meta made their billions as they encouraged us to freely give them all our data, and this also applies directly to AI tools. When you use a free tier of ChatGPT, Claude or similar services, you're effectively trading your data for access. They are using your prompt, the output of your prompt, the data you used to make that prompt work well, and lots of other metadata (your location, whether you were on a phone or computer etc) for their next model training run.

During one workshop, a participant shared that they'd been pasting entire client briefs into the free version of ChatGPT. They were shocked when I explained that this data would almost certainly be used to train the model, and they were likely breaching their client's NDA.

Most AI tools explicitly state in their terms that, if you are on their free plan (and sometimes their lower tier paid plans, too), they can use your inputs to improve their models. This means your confidential client information – brand strategies, campaign plans, product launches – could potentially be incorporated into the training data of a future model.

Many of the image generators are even worse. Any image you generate, along with the image prompt and any reference imagery, is automatically publicly displayed on their homepage by default, and is searchable by any user. Imagine you were creating mockups for a new brand and their pictures were popping up in every other Midjourney user's feed? The solution is straightforward:

1. **Move to paid professional plans:** ChatGPT Teams or Enterprise, and Claude Pro offer options where your data isn't used for training. If you're using Copilot through Office 365 or Gemini through a paid Google Workspace account you're fine. If you are using Midjourney, Ideogram or one of the other image generators, use a higher tier plan that allows you to turn on 'Private' or 'Stealth' mode.

2. **Check the terms and conditions:** Don't assume, always verify. Terms change frequently, so make it a habit to review them periodically.

I'm still slightly amazed at the number of agencies we go into where the majority of staff are still using free plans. Not only that, but the leadership team then complains they can't afford to roll out paid plans for them all. We have access to the most powerful technology we've ever seen for $30 per month per user – or even less if you're using Gemini through Google Workspace. Don't be cheap. If you don't think you can get $30 of value a month from these tools, then go back and re-read the earlier chapters of this book.

Copyright in the AI era: Who owns what?

The copyright landscape around AI-generated content remains unsettled, but there are some clear principles to follow. First, let's understand the fundamental issue: under current copyright law in Europe and America, copyright requires human creativity. Pure machine outputs aren't copyrightable because copyright law is anthropocentric – it requires a human creator. 'But what about the prompts I write?' a creative director asked during a recent workshop. 'Surely those are my creative input?' It's a good question, and the law is still evolving here.

But, on 28 January 2025, the US Copyright Office issued guidelines for copyright of AI works.[20] Their key guidelines were as follows:

1. **Prompts aren't copyrightable:** They're considered instructions, not original creative work.

2. **Outputs from AI tools aren't automatically protected:** The outputs of AI models are copyright free. To qualify for copyright, there needs to be clear evidence of human authorship in the final result. For instance, if you guide an image generator with a reference photo, and that reference is visibly reflected in the output, it may qualify.

3. **You can claim copyright if you modify the AI output:** If you take the generated content and apply your own creative input – such as editing the text or turning it into an advert by overlaying copy on an image – that modified version may be protected.

4. **Even AI-assisted edits can count – if they reflect human intent:** This includes using an AI tool for inpainting, where an AI modifies part of an image. As long as those changes were directed by human input, the result could be considered copyrightable.

In the UK, the Creative Industries Policy and Evidence Centre is taking this seriously and working to understand whether copyright should evolve in the age of AI.[21] Meanwhile, the UK Intellectual Property Office ran a public consultation from November 2024 to February 2025 and received over 11,000 responses – an unusually high number, which shows just how much interest and uncertainty there is around this topic.[22]

They're now analysing the feedback and have said they'll issue formal guidance by the end of 2025. My view? I'd be surprised if their approach ends up being radically different from what we're seeing in the US. The challenges are broadly the same, and there's a strong incentive for international alignment.

Here's what we do know for certain:

1. **Using an AI tool doesn't itself break copyright:** While the companies behind models like Midjourney may have broken copyright by training on images without permission, your use of the tool itself doesn't violate copyright law.

2. **If you generate something that infringes existing IP, that's still infringement:** Just because it came from an AI, doesn't mean you can generate Disney characters or use Nike's swoosh. Normal copyright rules still apply to what you create.

3. **To establish copyright on AI-generated work, you need to transform it:** Add your own creative input, modify the output in Photoshop, combine it with human-created elements, or otherwise transform the work sufficiently to qualify for human creative input.

What this means for your work

Here's the reality: if you want to own the intellectual property of what you create, you need to do something to those AI-generated images. Even something as simple as layering text over the image might make the combined file ownable under current copyright law.

Now, consider the implications. When you log into Midjourney and scroll through the public gallery, every image you see is a direct output of the AI model – and every single one is copyright free. Click on any image and you can see the exact prompt used to generate it, maybe even the reference image that guided it. You could legally take any of those pictures and use them for whatever you like. Or grab someone else's prompt and generate your own variation. Now imagine you're exploring creative concepts for a major client's upcoming campaign. Do you really want your experimental work visible to competitors, other agencies or anyone with a Midjourney account? Do you want someone to potentially use your creative exploration for their own purposes? The answer is obviously no. This is why ensuring you're on a plan that includes private mode isn't just nice to have – it's essential for client work. Your creative process should remain confidential until you choose to reveal it.

But the broader intellectual property question remains: if final ownership matters to you or your clients, you'll need to transform AI outputs in some meaningful way. The good news? This aligns perfectly with best practice anyway – AI generates compelling raw potential that needs professional human refinement to become truly effective work.

Be careful what you mimic

AI tools are remarkably good mimics. They've been trained on vast amounts of data – images, writing, music, design – and they're brilliant at picking up the stylistic fingerprints of different genres, periods and even individual creators. That's part of the magic: describe something well enough, and the AI will give you something that *feels* familiar. However, this ability to imitate so convincingly comes with some responsibility, too.

A growing number of creatives are using these tools to prompt in the style of specific authors, artists or filmmakers – often ones who are still living and working. While this might feel harmless, it's worth being honest about what's really happening: the line between inspiration and infringement is being tested every time you do it. Yes, some platforms are starting to add guardrails. OpenAI, Midjourney and others say you shouldn't prompt using specific names, but in reality, a lot still gets through. When GPT-4o's image generation was released, for instance, one of the big viral trends was creating images in the style of Studio Ghibli. The results were charming and nostalgic, but they also raised tough questions – because Ghibli's style is distinctive, copyrighted and part of a brand built up over decades.

Here's a better approach: if you want something in a particular style, describe the *style* – don't name the artist. Instead of asking for 'a pirate in the style of Captain Jack Sparrow', ask for 'an 18th-century pirate with flamboyant clothing, braided hair and a mischievous expression'. That way, you're tapping into the visual language you're after without dragging someone else's IP into it. The same applies across all creative fields – whether you're generating images, writing copy, composing music or designing ads. Don't be lazy, and treat other people's creative work with the same care and respect you'd want for your own. Just because the tools make it easy to mimic, doesn't mean it's the right thing to do.

Bias and the illusion of neutrality

When people talk about AI, there's often a casual assumption that it's neutral, impartial, objective. The truth is AI is anything but neutral. Because the data we feed it – the internet – is not neutral. It's packed with bias – historical bias, cultural bias, algorithmic bias. When you train a machine on biased data, you get a biased machine. Most large AI models – like ChatGPT, Midjourney and their cousins – are trained on huge swathes of content pulled from the public web. Think news sites, forums, blogs, Wikipedia, Reddit, Twitter, stock image archives, ecommerce product descriptions and more. That data reflects the world as seen through the lens of the internet.

And the internet, as we know, has an agenda. Not a conscious one, but a powerful one. It amplifies certain voices. It rewards certain aesthetics. It repeats certain ideas until they feel like facts. If we don't give an AI any specific direction and rely on its default view of the world, we'll get a view that reflects the internet. Its view of the world has been filtered through decades of digital distortion. If you ask an AI tool to show you what a CEO looks like, what do you expect to see? A woman in Lagos? A queer founder in their sixties? Someone in a wheelchair? Probably not. You'll likely get a clean-cut white man in a suit, possibly standing in a glass office tower, probably in New York or San Francisco. It's not because AI is sexist, racist or ageist on purpose; it's because AI is trained on the internet, and the internet is biased.

That's the heart of the issue. We've built a generation of tools that don't just process information – they reflect back to us a distorted image. AI doesn't show us the world as it is. It shows us the world as the internet depicts it. That world – online, filtered through algorithms, popularity contests and decades of unchecked content – isn't fair, balanced or diverse. It skews heavily toward what's most visible online: American voices, white faces, English-speaking content, youth culture, tech trends and recent data. That means the models we rely on – whether we're generating visuals, writing headlines or brainstorming new campaigns – are inherently tilted toward a fairly narrow worldview.

In a global creative economy, that's not just a quirk or an ethical issue. It's also a strategic risk. When you ask for a romantic couple, it might assume a straight couple. Ask for a 'typical family', and it'll likely give you a smiling mum, dad and two kids. Ask for a nurse, you'll probably get a woman. Ask for a scientist, you might get a man in a lab coat. None of this is a surprise if you've spent any time online – but it should still concern us. Because when we allow these patterns to dominate our creative outputs, we're not just copying culture. We're compounding its blind spots. The models aren't broken, they're doing exactly what they were designed to do: mimic patterns. The trouble is, the patterns are flawed.

The biggest danger is how subtle this all feels. AI-generated content doesn't scream bias. It whispers it, quietly, confidently, convincingly. A brand brief calls for 'a global team of creatives', and the AI gives you stock-photo-style visuals – diverse in skin tone, perhaps, but still filtered through a Western, polished lens. Everyone looks like they're dressed for a tech startup in Brooklyn. There are laptops, whiteboards, open-plan offices. It feels modern and familiar, but scratch the surface and you'll realise it's not truly global. It's globalised. Representation becomes aesthetic rather than authentic. If you don't stop and ask, 'Who's missing here?', you'll end up producing work that's subtly exclusionary, even when it's dressed up in inclusion.

For example, ask a generative AI to create an advert for a skincare product. Watch how quickly it defaults to clear-skinned, young, often white women with symmetrical faces. It's subtle, polished and algorithmically beautiful, but does it reflect your actual audience? Probably not. If you don't notice what's missing, your audience will. The same goes for voice. AI copy tends to favour clean, neutral, grammatically tidy English. But what about colloquial language? Cultural context? Humour? Rhythm? These are the soul of communication – and right now, they're still human things. AI can spark an idea, but it's your job to make sure the idea has legs – and a conscience.

So how do you tackle this in practice? You start by acknowledging it. Talk about it with your team. Make 'bias awareness' part of your creative process – not as a compliance box-tick, but as a craft discipline. Use AI for what it does best – iteration, exploration, speed – but never let it replace your judgement. If your team uses AI to storyboard, prompt them to test multiple perspectives. Don't just ask for 'a family dinner'. Ask for that scene across different cultures, income levels and geographies. See what changes. See what doesn't. These tiny moments of awareness – done consistently – reshape the entire quality of your output. Because in the end, creativity is not about what tools you use, it's about what you choose to show and who you choose to see. AI is not your creative director. It's your intern. A very clever, very fast but slightly untrustworthy intern. You can let it do the first round of work – but you must always review it, refine it, and ask, 'What truth are we putting into the world?' Because that's what the world will reflect back.

The environmental reality check

Walk into most creative agencies today and you'll hear the same whispered concern: 'Isn't ChatGPT terrible for the planet?' It's become the nagging voice in the back of many creative minds – that guilty feeling every time you fire up Midjourney or ask Claude to help refine a brief. Should we feel bad about using these tools? Are we contributing to some sort of environmental catastrophe with every prompt? The short answer? Your prompts aren't the problem. The reality is far more nuanced than the doom-laden headlines suggest. After digging deep into the latest research, here's what creative leaders actually need to know: the focus is often mistakenly put on individual AI use, but the real environmental impact comes from the infrastructure behind it – plus, enterprise systems that have been quietly running for years, not from the AI tools that grab all the attention.

Understanding the real environmental picture helps you make informed decisions about how and when to use AI most effectively. Perhaps more importantly, it helps you stop feeling guilty about using tools that can genuinely improve your creative work.

Your prompt isn't melting the polar ice caps

Let's start with the statistic that drives most headlines: a ChatGPT query uses roughly ten times more energy than a Google search. That sounds dramatic until you remember a single Google search is tiny – about 0.3 watt-hours, according to the International Energy Agency.[23] To put that in perspective, reading this chapter on your laptop for twenty minutes uses the same energy as six ChatGPT prompts. If everyone in the UK made ten AI queries daily for a full year, it would add just 0.2% to the country's total electricity consumption. For comparison, video streaming accounts for 1.5% of global electricity use – that's more than 1,600 times the energy consumption of ChatGPT.[24]

From a carbon footprint perspective, the numbers are equally tiny for individual users. Each ChatGPT query generates about two to five grams of CO_2. If you used ChatGPT ten times daily for an entire year, your carbon footprint would increase by about eleven kilograms of CO_2.[25] For the average UK resident with an annual carbon footprint of around seven tonnes, this represents a 0.16% increase.[26] Taking a one-hour commercial flight for a business meeting will increase your CO_2 emissions by more than prompting fifty ChatGPT queries a day for the rest of your life.

Water usage has become another flashpoint in AI environmental discussions, often generating misleading headlines.

The frequently cited statistic that 'ChatGPT uses 500 ml of water per query' is based on a fundamental misunderstanding. The original research found that 500 ml of water supported twenty to fifty queries, not individual ones.[27] Even this overstates the direct impact. When researchers examined the full water footprint of ChatGPT queries, they found that only 15% of the water was actually used in data centres themselves. The remaining 85% was water used in electricity generation – the same type of water consumption that powers every electrical device in your office.[28] Using industry methodology, a single ChatGPT query uses about 30 ml of water – roughly equivalent to sending an email. You can make about fifty ChatGPT queries for the equivalent water consumption of watching an hour of Netflix.

Where the real energy goes

Now that we've established how minimal individual use is, let's explore where AI's energy actually stacks up – and where creative leaders genuinely have influence. Consumer chatbots like ChatGPT, Claude and Gemini account for only about 3% of AI's total energy consumption.[29] The real energy users are the invisible systems we've been working within for years: recommendation engines powering Netflix suggestions and Amazon product recommendations, enterprise analytics used across industries for business intelligence, search and advertising algorithms processing billions of queries, computer vision systems analysing images and videos, and voice assistants like Alexa and Siri. This distinction matters enormously. Even if every single person stopped using ChatGPT tomorrow, it would barely register in AI's overall energy consumption. The systems driving

AI's environmental impact are largely invisible infrastructure that have been integrated into our digital lives for years.

Here's what matters most for creative leaders: many of these systems are shaped by your decisions. Whether you're a marketing director briefing a media campaign, a strategist working on customer segmentation, or a creative team designing digital experiences, you're not just an AI user – you're helping direct how and where AI is deployed at scale. While prompt-level awareness matters, real climate leadership in marketing and creative work means looking upstream and making more intentional choices about the infrastructure behind your work. You may not operate the servers – but you shape the demand. The same intentionality we apply at the prompt level can scale up to the systems we brief, fund and embed into daily workflows. Every decision to slow a refresh rate, simplify a brief or ask a vendor for carbon metrics makes a dent in the larger AI footprint. When those decisions happen at the scale of national campaigns, global platforms and growing startups, then they matter.

The environmental impact of AI infrastructure also needs weighing against the alternatives it might replace. If AI tools help reduce travel needs, optimise supply chains, accelerate scientific research or enable more efficient resource allocation, the net environmental impact could be positive.

How to think about your AI footprint

What does all this mean for agencies and marketing teams actively using AI tools?

Consider AI's lifecycle benefits. AI tools often help teams work more efficiently, potentially reducing the need for multiple revisions, extensive travel for research or resource-intensive alternative approaches. The environmental savings from these efficiencies could outweigh the direct energy costs. Focus on real impact. If you're serious about environmental responsibility, prioritise the areas where you can make genuine difference: energy-efficient office practices, sustainable travel policies, working with environmentally conscious clients, and advocating for clean energy infrastructure. Stay curious, too. The AI landscape evolves rapidly, and so does our understanding of its environmental implications. Keep track of developments, but don't let uncertainty paralyse you from using tools that can enhance your creative work.

The climate challenge is real and urgent, but it won't be solved by avoiding AI. It will be solved by clear thinking about where our energy actually goes – and using AI intentionally rather than wastefully. For creative leaders, that's liberating. Instead of second-guessing whether to use AI at all, invest in teaching your teams how to use it well. The biggest environmental wins come when well-trained people use AI to eliminate rework, serve clients more effectively and channel saved capacity into solving new challenges with fresh creativity. Use AI well, and it becomes part of the solution.

Key takeaways

- **The copyright foundation is uncomfortable but unavoidable.** All major AI models (with the exception of Adobe Firefly and Getty Images) were trained on copyrighted material without permission, creating an ethical tension you must acknowledge and decide how to navigate.

- **Don't be cheap.** Free AI tools make you the product. Using personal accounts for client work means your confidential briefs and brand strategies become training data for future models, almost certainly breaching client NDAs.

- **Pure AI outputs aren't copyrightable.** Under current law, you need to add meaningful human creative input to AI-generated content if you want to establish ownership and protect your work.

- **Mimicking specific artists crosses ethical lines.** Describe styles rather than naming creators to respect intellectual property and avoid reducing living artists' distinctive work to algorithmic patterns.

- **Bias reflects the internet's skewed worldview.** AI models amplify existing online biases around gender, race, geography and culture, requiring conscious intervention to ensure inclusive creative outputs.

- **Environmental impact is infrastructure, not individual use.** Your prompts consume minimal energy compared to enterprise systems, but thoughtful usage and awareness still matter for responsible adoption.

Your action point: Audit your AI tool stack

Spend thirty minutes conducting a comprehensive audit of every AI tool your team currently uses. Create an inventory listing all platforms (ChatGPT, Midjourney, Claude etc) and identify who's on free versus paid plans, then review each tool's terms and conditions to understand their data usage policies and storage locations. Upgrade any tools handling client data from free to professional plans that guarantee data protection, and document your entire setup in a simple one-page summary. By the end of this exercise, you should be able to confidently answer any client question about data privacy, security and where their information is stored – forming the foundation of the AI governance framework you'll need as clients become increasingly sophisticated about data protection.

PART 2
Building Your AI Strategy

8
The journey to AI maturity

More money is being poured into generative AI than any technology in human history. As a share of US GDP, it is more than double what was spent on the Apollo moon missions in the 1960s. This level of investment means the rate of improvement we've seen in generative AI models since they first went mainstream in 2022 shows no sign of slowing down.

For those of us running agencies, this means we have no choice but to decide how to work alongside AI. The choice isn't will I or won't I, it becomes how will I. Will you use AI primarily to reduce costs, risking a race to the bottom? Will you build AI capabilities that allow you to deliver your services on a bigger scale or at higher speed? Or will you use AI to push creative boundaries, developing customer experiences and connections for your clients that simply weren't possible before?

There is nowhere to hide from the fact that AI will commoditise certain tasks that creative professionals once built careers around. The ability to quickly generate serviceable copy, straightforward designs or functional videos will not command high fees for much longer. Yet at the same time AI allows creative teams to explore more options, improve the quality of their work and focus their creativity on the tasks that truly matter. As AI makes creating work that is 'good enough' accessible to many more people, our job as professionals is to create work that is exceptional – and use AI to help us create things that are better, and different, from what we did before.

This new reality requires us to make strategic choices. The agencies that will succeed in this new landscape won't necessarily be those with the most advanced AI tools or technical capabilities – although that will certainly help. The agencies that win will be the ones who develop a clear vision for how AI enhances their value proposition, who build thoughtful frameworks for integrating these tools into their workflows to deliver better client work, and who create cultures where human creativity and machine capabilities amplify each other. I'm convinced the winners won't be the ones who automate creativity; they will be the ones who amplify creativity.

In my mind, too many agencies are asking the wrong questions. They're thinking 'what's a good prompt for this' or 'what's the best tool for that'. In doing so, they are missing the wood for the trees. Cast your mind back to the late '90s, when the internet was beginning to really disrupt business, and it's the equivalent of asking whether you were better off using Netscape Navigator or Firefox as your web browser.

The four stages of AI maturity

When we launched Spark AI, we thought we'd find agencies neatly divided into two camps: those using AI and those who weren't.[30] The reality proved far more nuanced. After working with dozens of agencies and surveying where they were at the start of our Accelerator Programme and the trajectory they were on by the end, we've realised AI adoption follows a predictable path – one that every agency will eventually travel. We call it the AI Maturity Model, and it reveals exactly where your agency stands today and what you need to do next.

Stage 1: Experimentation – the Wild West phase

Your agency is in its earliest stage of AI adoption. Individual employees are exploring tools like ChatGPT or Midjourney independently. AI use is ad hoc, unstructured and driven by personal curiosity rather than strategic planning. Sarah from strategy mentions she's been using ChatGPT to help with research. Tom in creative shows off some Midjourney mood boards. Your finance director discovers that AI can help with analysing expense reports. Everyone's excited, but no one's quite sure what they're doing.

Here's what this looks like in practice:

- Employees self-teach AI tools, resulting in uneven use and skill levels.
- There's no formal strategy or alignment with business goals.
- People use basic AI tools in isolation for limited tasks.

- There's no agency-wide approach to tool selection or usage guidelines.

- Freelancers and contractors use AI without oversight.

- No one's accountable for driving progress – it's all voluntary enthusiasm.

The culture is cautious at best. Leadership recognises AI's potential but hasn't defined a vision or made it a priority. There's no structured discussion about how AI could impact future business opportunities, and certainly no budget allocated to proper implementation.

Most agencies start here. It's natural, it's human and it's completely understandable. It's also where most get stuck.

Stage 2: Adoption – getting serious

This is where AI stops being a novelty and starts becoming part of how you work. Leadership has defined a clear AI strategy aligned with operational goals. AI appears in team roadmaps and project plans. You're deliberately embedding AI in your core creative and strategic workflows to augment productivity and elevate quality across different functions. Structured policies, leadership alignment and training programmes ensure adoption spreads consistently across teams. Most importantly, you see AI as an enabler of higher-quality outputs and expanded creative capabilities.

Here's what this looks like in practice:

- An AI taskforce drives adoption with clear accountability.

- AI tools are integrated into creative workflows – ideation, research, prototyping.

- Structured training programmes ensure consistent AI proficiency across teams.
- Data is managed systematically with proper governance standards.
- Contracts ensure transparency with clients about AI use.

The cultural shift is palpable. Collaboration around AI becomes normal, with employees sharing use cases and insights. Recruitment and performance reviews start prioritising AI skills. The agency moves from wondering 'should we use AI?' to asking 'how can we use AI better?' This is where most forward-thinking agencies are today. It's a comfortable place to be – you're clearly ahead of the pack, delivering enhanced value to clients, and your team feels confident about the direction.

Stage 3: Optimisation – changing the way you work

Once you reach Stage 2: Adoption, you'll start to find your team spend their time on different tasks. Organisational structures and roles are reconfigured to reflect new workflows. Creating baseline outputs with AI becomes quick, so you invest the time saved in building out AI workflows, harnessing data to get better results and improving quality control to refine AI generated outputs.

AI becomes your operational backbone. You're not just using it to enhance human work – you're systematically identifying tasks that AI can handle semi-independently, then reorganising your team around these new capabilities.

Here's what this looks like in practice:

- Routine tasks across creative, client-facing and operational functions are largely automated.

- AI models are customised to agency and client-specific needs, with custom GPTs, ComfyUI workflows and other AI assistants in use across the business.

- Teams are restructured to align roles with AI capabilities, focusing on adding their unique expertise while overseeing partially automated processes.

- The skills mix changes as you train up or bring in employees who can build out your AI infrastructure.

- Close collaboration with clients on AI initiatives creates strong data partnerships.

The vision becomes clear: AI enables scaling operations and delivering high-quality outputs faster. You have long-term strategic plans focused on AI's transformative potential, and every major process includes AI as a standard component. This is where the economics really start to shift. You're not just working faster – you're working fundamentally differently.

Stage 4: Innovation – redefining what's possible

By this stage, AI has become integral to your agency's business model, driving innovation and creating entirely new forms of value. AI-powered products, services and client experiences position you as an industry leader, delivering long-term competitive advantages that competitors struggle to replicate. This is the promised land. AI doesn't just improve what you do – it enables you to do things that were previously impossible. You're creating new products and services, building proprietary capabilities on top of first party data, and fundamentally changing what clients expect from agencies.

Here's what this looks like in practice:

- AI transforms your value proposition, enabling new products and services.
- You deliver personalised, scalable, interactive experiences to your clients, and to their audiences.
- Advanced AI proficiency is embedded across all roles.
- An AI-first culture constantly unearths new opportunities.
- Data becomes a strategic asset, managed to optimise decision making.
- Bespoke AI tools unlock creative and operational possibilities.

Governance matures to focus on transparency, ethics and sustainable practices. Client contracts ensure full disclosure of AI use, fostering trust and deep collaboration. Your AI taskforce evolves into a strategic hub, driving innovation and setting industry standards. Nobody has reached Stage 4 yet, but the agencies that do will define what the creative industry looks like in five years' time. The agencies that are moving forwards are the ones that progress deliberately, building solid foundations at each stage before moving to the next. They understand that sustainable AI adoption requires changes in vision, culture, skills and governance – not just technology.

So where are you on the journey?

In March 2025, Emma, my Spark co-founder, and I gave a talk at an AI conference in the British Library to 150 agency leaders (organised by Ian Harris and the brilliant team at Agency Hackers). We'd recently published some market research looking at AI adoption in independent agencies, and we backed it up with a live poll on the day.

The 118 responses in the room closely mirrored our earlier findings from interviews: a little over 20% of agencies were deliberately moving forwards with AI. We called them AI Pioneers. They were building AI adoption programmes, implementing policies or guidelines and training up their staff. Some were even building their own tools. Meanwhile, 50% or so were stuck at the experimental stage – where AI use was largely down to individual initiative with little support to move beyond it. Amazingly for March 2025, there were still another 27% or so that weren't really doing anything with AI at all.

What we revealed was what separated the AI Pioneers from everyone else. The agencies that are getting this right have moved far beyond prompts and tools. They are thinking about all kinds of questions:

- Where does this create opportunities and risks for my business?

- How do my people gain the skills they need to use AI effectively?

- How do I manage my data to make it accessible to AI tools?

- How do I build repeatable ways of working across projects?
- How do I foster an AI-forward culture among my team?
- How do I keep my leadership accountable for driving our AI roadmap forwards?
- How do I talk to clients about this stuff without eroding my perceived value?

That's what this book is about. Not the technology itself – which will continue to evolve rapidly – but how to develop a strategic approach to AI adoption that strengthens rather than undermines what makes your agency special. Drawing on research with dozens of agencies at different stages of the AI journey, we'll explore practical frameworks for developing your AI strategy, upskilling your team, choosing the right tools and ultimately using AI to deliver more value to clients and work to power your business, not diminish it.

The goal isn't to turn your creative agency into a technology company. It's to ensure you can continue to do what creative agencies have always done best: delivering breakthrough ideas that help clients connect with their audiences – but now enhanced by capabilities that were once the stuff of science fiction but are now as accessible as turning on your iMac.

Key takeaways

- **The scale of investment is unprecedented.** More money is flowing into generative AI than any technology in human history ensuring the models are only going to get better and better.

- **The choice isn't whether to adopt AI, but how.** Agencies can use AI to cut costs (race to the bottom), scale operations (efficiency play) or push creative boundaries (innovation advantage).

- **AI will commoditise basic creative tasks.** Serviceable copy, straightforward designs and functional videos will no longer command premium fees, making exceptional work the new minimum standard.

- **Success comes from amplifying creativity, not automating it.** The winning agencies will be those that develop a clear vision for how AI enhances their value proposition.

- **Most agencies are asking the wrong questions.** Focusing on prompts and tools rather than strategic integration is like debating web browsers during the internet revolution.

- **AI adoption follows a predictable path.** The four stages go from Experimentation (scattered individual use) through Adoption (structured integration) and Optimisation (workflow transformation) to Innovation (new business models).

- **Only 20% of agencies are progressing strategically.** The majority remain stuck in experimental phases without systematic approaches to skills, data, culture or client communication.

- **The pioneers think beyond technology.** Successful agencies focus on business strategy, team development, data management, repeatable processes and client relationships rather than just tools.

Your action point: Assess your AI maturity

Take fifteen minutes to honestly assess where your agency sits on the AI Maturity Model. For each of the four stages, rate your current position on a scale of 1-10 across these dimensions: leadership strategy and vision, team skills and culture, data and tool integration, and governance and accountability.

Identify which stage best describes your overall position, then choose one specific area where you're weakest. This becomes your immediate focus area – whether that's establishing an AI taskforce, implementing structured training, developing data governance or creating client communication protocols.

The goal isn't to jump stages but to strengthen your foundations systematically. Book a two-hour session with your leadership team within the next month to discuss these findings and commit to specific next steps that move you closer to the next maturity stage. How do you do that? Read on.

9
Vision and strategy

Think back to the first big pitch you ever worked on. You were juggling endless tasks – pulling together audience data, reviewing different creative concepts, redrafting slides, running pricing scenarios – wondering if you'd ever get it all done in time. Looking back, I realise a lot of that effort was poured into repetitive tasks that could have been simplified. Back then, though, everything was done manually, and we felt proud of that 'hands-on' approach. Pulling an all-nighter was considered a badge of honour rather than the expected result of bad planning and last-minute decision making.

Fast-forward to today, and the first draft of the pitch can be generated by a custom GPT. Pricing options can be tailored to the personality of the buyers, and negotiating tactics practised with an AI persona. AI is reshaping our agencies in ways we couldn't have guessed back then. The hard part is understanding how.

Fortunately, we've created a simple way to understand how generative AI disrupts work, and a straightforward framework to apply it to your business, understand the likely impacts and opportunities, and build a plan towards it.

This chapter explores a framework to help you make sense of it all. Rather than being swamped by every new AI tool or headline, you can break down the possibilities and pitfalls using three categories: augmentation, automation and innovation. We'll then walk through an exercise that brings these ideas to life.

Understanding your agency's DNA

Before diving into how AI can transform your agency, you need to understand what makes your business special in the first place. AI should amplify your strengths, not replace your identity. What makes your agency special beyond just the services you provide? This question might seem basic, but it's fundamental to your AI strategy. You need to identify your unique selling propositions – those elements that make clients choose you over competitors.

Before we run our leadership workshops, we always ask the client team to step back and consider: what problem do you solve for your clients? Why do they come to you when there are hundreds of other agencies out there? What are they really buying from you?

It's easy for us to define our value by our *outputs* – we create brilliant visual identities, thoughtful strategies or beautiful adverts. However, AI forces us to reconsider our value in terms of *outcomes*. What is the client's ultimate objective, and how are we helping them achieve that?

Steve Edwards, one of our brilliant AI coaches and former agency founder, has a helpful challenge that captures this perfectly: 'Marketing directors don't want to buy branding or advertising – they want to buy sales. Ask yourself – how do you help them drive sales?'

One agency we worked with recently realised that their financial services clients weren't primarily buying their design skills – they were buying the agency's ability to translate complex products into simple, compliant communications that ordinary people could understand. This nuance changed how they approached their AI adoption. Once you've identified your superpower, how can AI enhance it?

Focus particularly on how you help clients achieve their goals. Do you make buying services easier? Do you provide differentiation in crowded markets? Do you build long-term sustained growth? What is the tangible business impact you deliver, beyond just the deliverables themselves. To truly understand your agency's DNA, you need to look through your clients' eyes. What problems are they really trying to solve when they come to you? A client might say they need a new website, but they might in fact be looking for:

- Greater relevance in their market
- A way to communicate complex offerings simply
- The confidence to pursue ambitious growth targets
- A distinct position against emerging competitors
- Building more engagement with their audiences

Look at your most successful client relationships. Why have they stayed with you? What keeps them coming back? Often, the official brief only scratches the surface of why clients truly value you.

Moving beyond deliverables to value

AI tools are starting to be able to produce many standard creative outputs quickly and cheaply, and this trend will only continue. It may not be long before traditional forms of creative production (building a website, conducting a video shoot, creating campaign assets) will cease to be a differentiator for most of us. This means you need to be crystal clear about where your real value lies.

Ask yourself:

- What outcomes are our clients truly after when they work with us?
- When clients recommend us, what do they say about us?
- Which aspects of our work would be hardest for competitors to replicate?
- What makes working with us different from working with other agencies?

Once you've identified these elements, try to articulate them simply. One helpful exercise is to complete this sentence: 'Clients come to us because we help them _____.'

Here are some example answers to this question from successful agencies:

- 'We help B2B brands become more memorable and meaningfully different, so they're chosen more often.'

- 'Clients come to us because we're in touch with their market, spot emerging trends and help them adapt and remain relevant.'

- 'We help clients make complex products easy to buy.'

These statements get to the heart of what you really do for clients, beyond service descriptions and deliverables.

Why this matters for AI adoption

Understanding your agency's DNA is crucial for effective AI adoption because it helps you identify opportunities. You'll see more clearly where AI can enhance your core value proposition rather than just making processes more efficient. It will also help you protect your differentiation: you'll recognise which elements of your work should remain human-centred, even as AI capabilities advance. You'll know where to direct your AI resources for maximum impact on what clients truly value. Finally, it will guide your messaging: you'll be able to communicate with clients about AI in a way that reassures rather than concerns them. Take time with your leadership team to discuss these fundamental questions about your business. The clearer you are about what makes your agency special, the more strategic you can be about how AI fits into your future. Remember, AI should amplify what makes you different, not dilute it. The agencies thriving with AI aren't using it to become more like everyone else – they're using it to become more distinctly themselves.

The AI Strategy Canvas™

Now that you understand what makes your agency special, it's time to map out how AI can enhance and extend these strengths. The AI Strategy Canvas is a practical tool I've developed to help agency leaders identify AI opportunities that align with their core business model.

Understanding the three AI opportunity types

The canvas divides AI opportunities into three categories, each with different implications for your business model:

Augmentation is where AI enhances your existing capabilities, helping your team work better and faster – creativity amplified, not automated. Think AI-assisted copywriting, mood-boarding and concepting, exploring design variations, creating prototypes and mockups or generating insights from research. The opportunities here focus on better-quality outputs, covering more ground and providing deeper exploration of creative options. However, these capabilities will become industry standard within a year or two, meaning early advantages are only temporary. Conversely, failing to adopt these working practices risks making you uncompetitive in the near future. Grammarly exemplifies this perfectly – an AI-powered writing assistant that allows a poor writer to create copy that's 'good enough', while helping a good writer sharpen their prose and accomplish more in the same time. It's not revolutionary, but it delivers better output and saves time for most copywriters. For £30 per month, who wouldn't want that?

Automation represents the next AI opportunity – machines taking over mundane tasks that require minimal human oversight. Think writing project status updates, conducting desk research, transcription and translation, drafting short-lived social posts, certain kinds of web development, subtitling a video or resizing assets for different platforms. As the technology improves, more tasks will inevitably fall into this category. The opportunities are obvious: cost savings, efficiency gains and freeing up your team's time for higher-value work. However, automation comes with a downside too – services that can be automated will become commoditised over time, creating severe downward pressure on pricing. Take RWS, a localisation service for the media industry that helps caption, translate and dub films, TV shows and adverts. LLMs turned out to be surprisingly good translators, able to transcribe video with 95% accuracy in minutes, making it simple for a native speaker to proofread and correct. Since ChatGPT launched in November 2022, RWS's share price has halved.[31] Kate Ross's experience with AI efficiency gains is telling:

> 'We pretty much hand all the AI productivity savings over to the client. Otherwise, what's the point? Might as well do it the traditional way. We're not making extra profit from it. It's about staying relevant and competitive in the market. It's definitely not a money maker.'

Innovation is the hardest part. This is where AI enables entirely new services or business models that weren't practical before – data-driven personalisation, interactive AI-powered brand experiences, or solutions we haven't yet imagined. What would a brilliant experience for your client look like? What would transform their customers' experience? How can AI help you deliver that? Many innovative applications remain hard to picture right now, like trying to predict Facebook, Uber or Airbnb's business models back in the 1990s. The opportunities include new revenue streams, differentiation and sticky client relationships, but the risks are real – the future remains unclear, requiring experimentation and investment in capabilities that may take time to perfect and sell. Duolingo demonstrates this perfectly. While LLMs could have commoditised their language learning app (they're surprisingly good translators and teachers), Duolingo thought strategically about what learners really needed – practice with native speakers – and used AI to create exactly that. Their AI avatar Lily, combined with an enhanced learning experience, has made the app stickier than ever. Duolingo's share price has risen 20% since ChatGPT's launch.[32] The same technology commoditising RWS became Duolingo's source of differentiation. That's how to think like a pioneer.

Creating your AI Strategy Canvas

Here's a detailed exercise you can run with your team, bringing these three categories – augmentation, automation and innovation – together in a single conversation.

1. **Gather everyone:** Invite colleagues from all parts of your agency: client services, strategy, creative, production, plus people from finance or IT.

2. **Brainstorm tasks and roles:** Split everyone into groups, each focusing on a specific function (eg production, research and strategy). Hand out sticky notes (or open a shared digital space – we use Miro) and ask each team to list their everyday tasks. Encourage them to be honest and

detailed: everything from scheduling social posts to high-level brand strategy.

3. **Use the matrix:** Complete the following table by placing each task where you think it belongs and colour-code each one – mark potential risk (red), requirement (yellow) or advantage (green). For instance, if your production team does a lot of background removal, you might mark that as high risk (red) if you don't plan to automate it soon.

	Client services	Research & strategy	Creative	Production	Support services
Augmentation					
Automation					
Innovation					

4. **Compare notes:** Reconvene as a single group. One by one, talk through each function's sticky notes.

5. **Evaluate current services for vulnerability:** Which of your services could be most easily automated by clients using AI tools themselves? Which of these tasks currently consume disproportionate time? Are these internal processes or client-facing services? If client-facing, how will you handle the potential commoditisation? Are there tasks here that eat up a lot of the team's time or justify a chunk of your fees?

6. **Identify augmentation opportunities:** How can you use AI to make your core services dramatically better in ways clients would value? How will this improve your core value proposition? Will this allow you to deliver better

outcomes or just work faster? How will you continue to differentiate when competitors adopt similar capabilities? Do you need new tools, training or workflows?

7. **Explore innovation possibilities:** What previously impossible services could you now offer that align with your agency's DNA? How does this connect to what clients already value about you? What new client problems could this solve? What capabilities would you need to develop to deliver this? Is there a pilot project you could try next quarter?

The implications of the AI Strategy Canvas for your business

Your AI Strategy Canvas reveals more than just opportunities – it exposes fundamental shifts coming to your business model that demand proactive responses. As AI augmentation accelerates your work and transforms your services, your pricing approach must evolve accordingly. The traditional time-based billing model becomes increasingly untenable when machines can accomplish in minutes what once took hours. Instead, consider transitioning towards value-based pricing for strategic work, outcome-based pricing where results are measurable, product-like pricing for scalable AI-enabled solutions, or subscription models for ongoing AI-enhanced services that deliver continuous value rather than one-off deliverables.

Equally significant are the implications for how you structure your team. Your canvas will illuminate which roles need to evolve as AI handles more routine aspects of their work, what new capabilities you'll need to develop or acquire to take advantage of emerging opportunities, and how teams might be reorganised around AI-enabled workflows that blur traditional departmental boundaries. This isn't about replacing people, it's more about reimagining how human expertise combines with machine capabilities to create something more powerful than either could achieve alone.

Consider a B2B agency specialising in marketing complex services. Their AI Strategy Canvas might reveal that much of their production work – basic copywriting, standard layouts – faces automation, threatening a significant revenue stream. However, AI could also dramatically improve their creative ideation process, enabling exploration of more concepts and territories for clients in highly regulated industries. Most intriguingly, they might discover an opportunity to create an entirely new offering: an AI-powered brand compliance system ensuring all marketing materials stay within regulatory guidelines while maintaining creative impact. Based on this analysis, they could begin building AI enhancement into the production process to increase quality and volume without increasing costs, charge premium prices for AI-augmented creative concepting that showcases broader exploration across more media, and invest in developing their brand compliance platform as a new subscription service offered to financial services clients. The result isn't just operational improvement – it's business model evolution that positions them ahead of competitors still thinking in traditional terms.

Remember, the most valuable part of this exercise isn't just identifying what AI can do at a technical level, but understanding how it can enhance what makes your agency special.

Your goal isn't to become an 'AI agency' – it's to become an even better version of the agency you already are, using AI as a powerful enabler. The real question is whether you're proactive in adopting and shaping these changes, or whether you wait until the market forces your hand. The augmentation – automation – innovation framework and the team exercise allow you to map out the present and future of your agency in a tangible, honest way. Instead of vague predictions, you can identify specific tasks that are ripe for automation, areas where you must bring in new AI-assisted workflows to keep up, and the inventive ideas that could separate you from the pack. Remember, it's not about robots versus people. It's about how we use AI to free ourselves from routine tasks, enhance our thinking and drive our ambitions forward. If you're anything like me, you'll look back on these changes in a couple of years and see how they gave your agency more room to shine, letting you focus on the creative spark that first drew you into this industry.

From big ideas to specific projects

Now that you've mapped potential AI opportunities across your agency using the Strategy Canvas, it's time to get specific. The difference between agencies that talk about AI and those that successfully implement it often comes down to how well they define their initiatives.

The opportunities you've identified in your canvas are likely broad in scope. To move forward effectively, you need to translate them into well-defined initiatives with clear boundaries and success metrics. For example, 'using AI to enhance our creative work' is too vague to act upon. A more specific initiative might be: 'Implement an AI-augmented conceptual development process that allows us to explore double the number of creative territories in the same timeframe'. Let's look at how to define initiatives that will move your agency forward. Start by reviewing the opportunities you identified in your AI Strategy Canvas. For each area of your business, select the ideas that seem most promising and develop them into more concrete initiatives. Here's what this might look like for each function.

Client services

- Create an AI-assisted brief development system that synthesises client requirements, past work and market insights.

- Develop an automated project status reporting system that pulls from project management tools.

- Build a client onboarding process that uses AI to customise materials to each client's industry and needs.

Research and strategy

- Implement an AI-powered competitor analysis system that monitors key competitors and provides monthly insights.

- Create a streamlined research synthesis process that combines a range of data sources into actionable strategies.

- Develop a distinctive brand-asset evaluation tool to help clients quantify their brand's memorability.

Creative

- Design an AI-augmented creative exploration process that generates varied conceptual approaches based on strategy inputs.

- Create a brand voice calibration system that ensures all content aligns with established tone-of-voice guidelines.

- Develop a conceptual stress-testing tool that evaluates creative ideas against strategic objectives and audience needs.

Production

- Build an automated asset adaptation system that creates variations for different channels and formats.

- Implement an AI-enhanced quality control process that checks deliverables against brand guidelines and best practices.

- Develop a rapid prototyping workflow that accelerates the creation of web and app mockups.

Support services

- Create an HR policy chatbot that allows colleagues to answer straightforward questions about holiday allowance or maternity cover themselves.

- Implement natural language in your financial reporting that allows project managers to get real-time insights on project profitability.

- Develop a recruitment screening process that identifies candidates with the right skills.

New business

- Build a prospecting system that identifies and prioritises potential clients based on fit and win probability.

- Create an AI-enhanced pitch preparation process that customises case studies and approaches to each prospect.

- Develop a capability demonstration platform that showcases your AI-enabled workflows to potential clients.

Prioritising your initiatives: The 3S Framework

Not everything can be done at once. Once you've defined a range of potential initiatives, you need to prioritise them. Trying to pursue too many at once is a recipe for failure. The 3S Framework helps you evaluate and rank your initiatives based on three key dimensions:

1. **Size of opportunity:** How significant is the potential impact on your business or your clients? Consider factors such as:
   - Revenue impact (will this increase income or protect existing revenue?)
   - Cost savings (will this reduce expenses or improve efficiency?)
   - Strategic importance (will this strengthen your competitive position?)
   - Client value (will this significantly enhance what you deliver to clients?)

2. **Speed:** How quickly and easily can the initiative be implemented? Consider:
   - Technical complexity (does this require specialised expertise?)
   - Dependencies (does this rely on other systems or changes first?)
   - Resource requirements (how much time and money will this take?)
   - Learning curve (how easily can your team adapt to this change?)

3. **Scale:** How widely applicable is the solution to different clients and situations? Consider:
   - Versatility (can this be used across multiple client types or sectors?)
   - Adaptability (can this be customised for different needs?)
   - Growth potential (can this be expanded over time?)
   - Reusability (will this create assets, learnings or capabilities you can leverage for other opportunities in the future?)

Using this framework, you can score each initiative and create a prioritised list. Don't overthink it. A simple high, medium or low marked against each dimension is probably enough. We're not looking for detailed business cases here, simply a way to filter down dozens of ideas into the top two or three you'll work on next. Initiatives that score highly across all three dimensions should generally be your first priorities. However, it's also worth considering a balanced portfolio approach. Think about one initiative in each category below so you can spread risk:

- A quick win (high speed) to build momentum
- A strategic investment (high size) to secure long-term advantage
- A broadly applicable capability (high scale) to maximise return on investment

Measuring success: Defining some metrics for AI initiatives

Traditional return on investment calculations often struggle with AI initiatives, as there are few precedents on which to base your valuation. Instead, consider a broader range of metrics tailored to the goal of AI implementation.

For augmentation initiatives:

- **Quality improvement:** Develop metrics that assess output quality. For example, 'Average number of amends reduced from 2.3 to 1.5'.
- **Exploration breadth:** Measure the range of options explored. For example, 'Now exploring an average of eight creative territories per brief vs. three previously'.
- **Speed to value:** Track time to deliver meaningful outcomes. For example, 'Reduced time to first concept presentation by 40%'.
- **Client feedback:** Gather structured feedback on improved outputs. For example, '60% of clients report receiving more strategically aligned creative work'.

- **Win rate:** Monitor impact on competitive situations. For example, 'Pitch-win rate increased from 30% to 45%'.

For automation initiatives:

- **Time saved:** Measure the reduction in hours spent on tasks. For example, 'Reduced time spent on meeting notes by 75%'.
- **Cost reduction:** Calculate direct financial savings. For example, 'Decreased production costs for basic assets by 40%'.
- **Volume capacity:** Measure increased output. For example, 'Doubled the number of social media assets we can produce monthly'.
- **Error reduction:** Track improvements in accuracy. For example, 'Reduced brand guideline violations by 90%'.
- **Employee satisfaction:** Survey team members about the impact on their role. For example, '85% of designers report spending more time on creative work they enjoy'.

For innovation initiatives:

- **New revenue:** Track income from new AI-enabled services. For example, 'Generated £120K in the first year from our personalisation platform'.
- **Client retention:** Measure impact on client relationships. For example, 'Increased our win rate from 30% to 45%'.
- **Premium pricing:** Monitor your ability to charge higher fees. For example, 'Command 15% higher fees for AI-enhanced strategy work'.

- **Market differentiation:** Assess competitive advantage through client surveys. For example, '65% of clients cite our AI capabilities as a key differentiator'.

- **Business development impact:** Track influence on new business. For example, 'AI capabilities mentioned in 70% of incoming enquiries'.

For each initiative you select, identify a couple of key metrics that will best measure your level of success. Establish baseline measurements before implementation so you can track your progress. We're not looking to create a cottage industry here, but you want to be able to understand if the initiative is moving you towards your goal or not.

As you refine these ideas, ensure that each initiative:

- Has a clear scope and well-defined boundaries
- Delivers a specific benefit to your agency or to your clients
- Can be implemented within a reasonable timeframe
- Has measurable outcomes

As one agency leader quoted in our research for our Accelerator Programme noted:

> 'What's measured gets managed. When we started tracking the impact of our AI initiatives specifically, rather than just as part of general business performance, we could see which approaches were genuinely moving the needle.'

Start building your AI roadmap

Once you've selected your two or three priority initiatives using the 3S Framework, it's time to integrate them into a practical roadmap. This doesn't need to be complex – in fact, simplicity is key to successful implementation. Your roadmap should convert your strategic thinking into clear actions with responsibility assigned to specific people or teams. For each initiative:

- **Assign clear ownership:** Who is accountable for making this happen? This person doesn't need to do all the work themselves, but they must drive the initiative forward.

- **Define a realistic timeline:** When will you start this initiative and by when should it be completed? Be realistic about dependencies and available resources.

- **Set key milestones:** What are the critical checkpoints along the way? These serve as progress indicators and decision points.

- **Establish success metrics:** How will you know if the initiative is successful? Define two or three metrics that align with the type of initiative (automation, augmentation or innovation).

Making your roadmap work

To ensure your roadmap delivers results:

1. **Start with a manageable number of initiatives:** Two or three is ideal for your first wave. Don't try to transform everything at once.

2. **Balance quick wins with strategic initiatives:** Include at least one initiative that will show results within a month or two to build momentum and demonstrate value.

3. **Consider dependencies:** Sequence initiatives logically, building foundational capabilities before more advanced applications.

4. **Distribute responsibility:** Spread ownership across different parts of the business to avoid overburdening any one person or team.

5. **Align with business cycles:** Time major implementations to avoid your busiest periods.

6. **Review regularly:** Schedule monthly check-ins to track progress, address challenges and make adjustments as needed.

7. **Celebrate and communicate successes:** Share wins broadly to maintain enthusiasm and demonstrate the value of your AI strategy.

Remember that your roadmap is a living document. As you learn what works and what doesn't, you'll need to adjust your plans. The goal isn't the perfect execution of the original plan – it's having a meaningful impact on your agency and your clients. Schedule a review in three or six months. When I've run these sessions, I've found that some tasks move more quickly than expected (for example, it's just become a new feature in Adobe Firefly), while others require more cultural or process shifts. By revisiting your matrix, you keep the momentum going and remain alert to new tools and market changes.

Key takeaways

- **Start with your agency's DNA, not the technology.** Understand what your clients truly value about working with you before mapping out how AI can amplify those strengths rather than dilute them.

- **The AI Strategy Canvas reveals three distinct opportunity types.** These are augmentation (AI enhances human work), automation (AI takes over tasks), and innovation (AI enables entirely new services). Each of these has different business implications.

- **Augmentation becomes table stakes within twenty-four months.** AI-enhanced capabilities will quickly become the industry standard, making adoption essential to avoid becoming uncompetitive.

- **Automation brings efficiency but risks commoditisation.** Tasks that can be largely automated will face severe downward pricing pressure, threatening traditional revenue streams.

- **Innovation creates sustainable competitive advantage.** Entirely new AI-enabled services and business models offer the greatest potential for differentiation and premium pricing.

- **The 3S Framework cuts through AI overwhelm.** Prioritise initiatives based on the size of the opportunity, the speed of implementation and the scale of application, so you can focus your energy on highest-impact activities.

- **Specific initiatives beat vague aspirations.** Transform broad AI opportunities into concrete projects with clear owners, realistic timelines and measurable success metrics.

- **Your roadmap must balance quick wins with strategic investments.** Include initiatives that show immediate results alongside longer-term capabilities that create lasting competitive advantage.

> **Your action point: Complete your personal AI Strategy Canvas**
>
> Take half an hour to have a quick think through the AI Strategy Canvas exercise for your own agency. Draw a simple table with your key business functions (eg New Business, Creative, Strategy, Client Services, Production) as columns, and the three opportunity types (augmentation, automation, innovation) as rows. For each intersection, write one specific example of how AI could impact that function, then mark it as a risk (red), requirement (yellow), or advantage (green). Finally, circle the three opportunities that score highest on the 3S Framework – size, speed and scale. The ones that score the highest become your priority AI initiatives and the foundation for building your agency's transformation roadmap.

10
People, skills and culture

The most powerful technology on the planet is now available for less than the cost of a sandwich in central London. The basic plan on ChatGPT is free, and Midjourney is £8 per month. The technology is no longer the barrier to entry. What separates the agencies that will thrive using AI from those that merely survive is what they do with it. It's about the people who use these tools, the skills they develop and the culture that enables them to innovate.

Right now, your biggest AI challenge isn't technological – it's psychological. During our research for the *AI in Creative Industries 2025* report, between autumn 2024 and spring 2025, we surveyed 150 agency professionals about their AI adoption barriers.[33] The responses were telling.

- 67% cited 'not knowing how to apply AI to my specific role'.
- 52% mentioned 'not having time to experiment properly'.

- 41% worried about 'maintaining creative authenticity'.
- 38% felt 'overwhelmed by the pace of AI development'.

Notice what's missing? Nobody mentioned cost. Nobody complained about access to tools. The barriers are entirely human: imagination, time, confidence and culture. This creates an extraordinary opportunity. While your competitors obsess over which AI platform to buy, you can leap ahead by focusing on the thing that actually matters: helping your people understand how these tools amplify their existing talents. The agencies leading the AI revolution aren't necessarily the ones with the biggest budgets or the most advanced technical resources. They're the ones that are successfully engaging their people in the journey, creating a culture of continuous learning, and developing the skills needed to apply these powerful tools to client challenges. The good news is that cultivating an AI-forward team doesn't cost anything. However, it does require thoughtful leadership, clear direction and practical approaches to bringing your people along on the journey. Unlike technology, which is widely available to all, your unique combination of people, skills and culture can't be easily replicated by competitors.

Assembling your AI taskforce

Even the most brilliant AI strategy will fail without someone to drive it forward. This is where your AI taskforce comes in – a dedicated group responsible for championing AI adoption and ensuring it delivers real value for your agency and clients. An AI taskforce isn't just another committee or working group, it's a catalyst for change with specific responsibilities that help transform how your agency works with AI.

Think of your taskforce as the connecting tissue between high-level AI strategy and day-to-day implementation. They're the ones who drive adoption, helping colleagues embrace new tools and workflows. They set standards and establish guidelines for responsible AI use. They curate knowledge, building repositories of best practices, prompts and training resources. They solve problems, addressing obstacles that arise during implementation. They also keep an eye on the horizon, monitoring relevant developments that might benefit your agency.

When you see an agency with an effective taskforce in action, you'll notice focused experimentation rather than scattered efforts. New AI approaches move smoothly from conception to implementation, and there's a growing library of agency-specific AI resources. Perhaps most importantly, you'll see your team's confidence increase as they incorporate AI into their daily work, supported by a structure that encourages learning while maintaining quality standards.

Within thirty days of establishing your taskforce, you should have initial guidelines and training resources in place. By ninety days, you should see adoption spreading beyond the early enthusiasts. Within six months, AI workflows should be normalising across most teams.

Identifying key members and their responsibilities

The right composition for your taskforce will depend on your agency's size and structure, but there are some key principles to follow.

For smaller agencies (under thirty people), a taskforce of four or five people is typically sufficient. Larger agencies (100 people and up) might expand to six to ten members. You want a mix of strategic thinkers who understand the agency's vision and your clients' needs as well as practical implementers who can translate ideas into workable processes. Different levels of seniority will help provide varied perspectives on challenges. When it comes to specific roles, consider including:

- An **AI Sponsor.** Typically, this will be a senior leader who champions AI adoption across the agency and sets the overall direction of your AI programme. This person secures resources, provides strategic direction and ensures AI initiatives align with the goals of the business. They need the authority to make decisions and remove roadblocks. This will often be the founder, MD or CEO.

- An **AI Lead.** This will be your AI programme manager. They don't need to be an AI expert, but they do need to be action-oriented, have strong organisational skills and be able to build a plan and make others stick to it.

- A **Technical Lead.** This will be someone who's comfortable with the more technical aspects of AI. This isn't about finding a coding genius; rather, you want someone who understands how AI works and who enjoys getting their hands dirty. They'll be your go-to person for evaluating new tools, overseeing the creation of AI assistants and ensuring your data is AI-ready.

You'll also want representatives from different functions – people from creative, strategy, client services or other key departments. These individuals identify opportunities in their areas and help implement changes. They're your eyes and ears on the ground, spotting where AI can make the biggest difference.

Watch out for these common pitfalls:

- Creating a taskforce on paper but never giving members dedicated time to do the work
- Filling your taskforce exclusively with technical people and missing the creative perspective
- A taskforce that works in isolation without regular engagement with the wider team
- Perhaps worst of all, a group with enthusiasm but no actual authority to implement changes

When selecting people for these roles, look beyond their technical skills. Genuine interest and enthusiasm for AI often matter more than existing expertise. You want a mixture of people who are respected by their peers and whose opinions carry weight across the agency, but also some who are fresh enough to reimagine how things can be done and are not stuck in their ways. I teach many of the principles in this book at Oxford University for their postgraduate diploma for AI in Business. One executive in a recent cohort told me how his organisation, a large bank, had recruited half their AI taskforce members from their graduate recruitment pool. He felt that senior executives like him were often unable to imagine how things could be different.

Finally, you need a growth mindset in the team – being open to learning and comfortable with ambiguity is essential in a field that changes weekly. Don't forget to include diverse perspectives; different backgrounds, experience levels and thinking styles will strengthen your approach.

Developing an AI adoption charter

To set your taskforce up for success, create a simple charter that outlines their purpose and responsibilities. This doesn't need to be a lengthy document – a single page will do. Your charter should cover the taskforce's purpose (why it exists and what it aims to achieve), scope (the boundaries of their responsibilities), authority (what decisions they can make independently), composition (who's involved and their specific roles), and operating model (how the taskforce will work day-to-day).

Want a shortcut? Here's a prompt to generate your taskforce charter:

> Create an AI Taskforce Charter for my agency. Ask me five relevant questions, one at a time. Following my interview, draft the charter. Include sections for:
>
> - Purpose and objectives
>
> - Scope of responsibilities
>
> - Decision-making authority
>
> - Composition and roles
>
> - Operating model (meeting frequency, reporting structure)
>
> Keep it concise (one page) but specific to our context. Focus on practical implementation rather than theoretical exploration.

The charter should clarify what the taskforce is authorised to do without further approval – perhaps they can recommend agency-wide tools, implement new workflows, allocate a designated AI training budget and make recommendations on AI strategy. The composition section lists your specific taskforce members and their roles, while the operating model might specify bi-weekly taskforce meetings, monthly updates to leadership, quarterly all-staff AI updates and an annual review of priorities. A charter like this creates clarity from the outset and prevents the taskforce from becoming just another talking shop.

Setting the taskforce up for success

Even the most enthusiastic taskforce will struggle without the right support. I've seen this happen repeatedly – agencies create a taskforce with great fanfare, but they quickly become ineffective without proper backing.

First and foremost, taskforce members need dedicated time to fulfil their responsibilities. This might be a set percentage of their working week, specific days allocated to taskforce activities, or their other responsibilities could be adjusted. Be explicit about this allocation and treat it as protected time. This is by far the hardest part of everything in this book. Safeguarding a couple of hours a week for the taskforce to actually run your AI programme will be the most important thing you can do to drive it forwards. If you want things to change, then you have to change things.

But with this time commitment comes accountability. Establish clear expectations for what the taskforce will deliver and by when. What should they accomplish in their first thirty to ninety days? What are their medium-term objectives for the next three to six months? What are their long-term goals for the year ahead? These expectations should align with your AI roadmap and be realistic given the time they have been allocated.

Provide the resources needed for success. This includes budget for the relevant AI tools and platforms, some budget – or at least time – for training and development, and the authority to experiment with new approaches. This doesn't need to be extensive – even a modest budget can enable significant progress if used strategically; AI tools are not expensive in the grand scheme of things. Also ensure the taskforce has visible support from senior leadership through regular check-ins, participation in key initiatives and public endorsement of their work. This signals to the wider agency that AI adoption is a strategic priority, not a side project. Finally, create channels for the taskforce to gather input from across the agency – regular feedback sessions, open forums for discussing AI challenges, and simple ways for anyone to suggest new AI applications. This helps identify obstacles early and builds broader engagement with AI initiatives.

Cultivating an AI-forward culture

Your AI strategy will live or die based on culture, not technology. When I ask agency leaders about their biggest AI implementation challenges, the answers are rarely about capabilities or costs – they're almost always about people and priorities. The real barriers are refreshingly practical. First, there's the perpetual time crunch. Everyone's maxed out on client work and existing responsibilities. 'We'd love to explore AI more, but when?' is a common refrain. Second, there's a surprisingly widespread imagination gap. People simply don't know how these tools could apply to their specific role or challenges. They see impressive demos but struggle to connect them to Monday morning's workload. What does genuine cultural transformation look like? It's when AI shifts from being an exotic special project to becoming simply 'how we work'. It's when your team stops seeing AI as something separate that requires extra time and starts recognising it as something that creates time by enhancing efficiency and capability.

You'll know you're succeeding when AI naturally weaves itself into everyday conversations. When a strategist casually mentions, 'I ran three different audience analyses through Claude before finalising my recommendations.' When a designer shows a creative director multiple concept directions and receives the question, 'Have you explored how Midjourney might visualise this from another angle?' When project timelines automatically include AI exploration phases because everyone recognises their value. One of the characteristics of the AI Pioneers is how they've made AI part of the normal workflow by carving out dedicated time for exploration and, crucially, by creating concrete examples of how these tools apply to every role in the agency.

Your challenge is to transform AI from 'one more thing we should be doing' into something your team reaches for instinctively because it solves real problems they face every day. This isn't about adding AI to people's plates – it's about using AI to help them do what's already on their plates more effectively, creatively and enjoyably.

Encouraging experimentation

One powerful thing you can do to accelerate AI adoption is to create an environment where experimentation isn't just allowed – it's celebrated. I've seen countless agencies stuck in paralysis because people are up against client deadlines and are too afraid the new tools will fail them, so they stick to the time-tested methods they already know. Your job is to shatter that fear. Start by carving out dedicated exploration time. One agency I work with implemented what they call 'AI Fridays' – a sacred two-hour window where team members experiment with AI tools with zero expectation of client-ready output. Within just four weeks, they traced three new ways of working directly back to these sessions. Why? Because their people could play, fail, discover and iterate without the pressure of immediate delivery.

You need to lead by example here. When was the last time you shared your own attempts at mastering a new AI technique? When leaders openly discuss their learning journeys – including the occasional blind alley – it gives everyone permission to do the same. Make learning visible by starting each team meeting with a five-minute AI discovery share. Keep it brief and specific – a clever prompt technique, a new feature someone's discovered or an unexpected application that saved hours on a project. This simple ritual signals that continuous learning is part of your culture, not an optional extra. When recognising progress, celebrate improvement over mastery. The person who's moved from complete AI avoidance to basic competence has often made a more significant leap than your power user who's refined an already strong skill. Make heroes of those who overcome their reluctance and embrace the learning curve.

PEOPLE, SKILLS AND CULTURE

I've watched too many agencies sabotage their own efforts by setting invisible barriers to experimentation. They say all the right things about innovation but never actually block out time for it. They expect top-notch results from first attempts. They let anxiety-driven conversations dominate instead of balancing legitimate concerns with exciting possibilities. Most dangerously, they allow AI to become the exclusive domain of a self-selected elite. Experimentation shouldn't just be free time; tie it directly to project work. Pick a project you ran last month. How would you do that again using AI to help you? This approach works well because it allows you to work on real client work, but without the deadline. As you've already done the work the traditional way, it gives you a clear benchmark of what good looks like and how long it took to get there. Your challenge is to democratise experimentation – making it accessible, expected and embedded in your weekly rhythm rather than an occasional activity. When experimentation becomes as normal as checking email, you'll know you're on the right track.

Implementing a buddy system

I've seen agencies struggle for months with formal training programmes only to transform their capabilities in weeks once they implement a simple buddy system. Your first task is to identify your natural AI champions – those people who light up when discussing these tools and are already exploring them in their own work. Don't make assumptions about who these people are. I've seen junior designers teach creative directors game-changing prompt techniques, and sixty-year-old copywriters become the resident ChatGPT experts. Enthusiasm for

AI cuts across all traditional hierarchies and often comes from unexpected corners. Pair these champions thoughtfully with colleagues who could benefit from hands-on guidance. The magic happens when you frame this not as remedial help but as collaborative exploration. A design director at one of London's top agencies told me: 'We turned our buddy system into a series of "AI challenges" where pairs competed to solve client problems in new ways. What started as teaching became genuine collaboration within days.'

The golden rule of effective buddy systems is ruthless practicality. Focus exclusively on applying AI to real work – not theoretical capabilities or impressive demos. When a junior copywriter sees their mentor use ChatGPT to generate ten headline options for an actual client pitch in three minutes, the lightbulb moment is immediate and powerful. The timeline for results will surprise you. Within four weeks, you'll typically see significantly increased confidence and independent usage among those who were initially hesitant. By three months, many of your 'buddies' will be independently exploring new applications. I frequently see a complete role reversal within six months, with original learners becoming teachers for the next wave of adoption.

Spend twenty minutes mapping your team across two dimensions: AI enthusiasm (high to low) and influence within the agency (high to low). Create a simple grid and place each team member's name in the appropriate quadrant.

Your high-enthusiasm, high-influence people become your AI taskforce candidates. Your high-influence sceptics need individual conversations to understand their concerns. Your enthusiastic juniors become perfect candidates for your buddy system. This exercise reveals exactly who should drive your AI adoption, who needs special attention and how to leverage existing relationships to accelerate culture change across your entire agency.

Fostering ownership

One of the key differences between agencies where AI is a passing fad and those where it becomes transformative is ownership. When AI tools remain the domain of a central 'innovation team' or a few tech enthusiasts, they never fully integrate into your agency's DNA.

Your AI taskforce shouldn't do all the work themselves. Members of the taskforce should delegate down to their teams and distribute AI ownership deliberately across your agency, embedding it into people's core responsibilities rather than treating it as an add-on. Start by mapping specific AI responsibilities to people's natural interests and existing roles. Your senior copywriter who's always been passionate about tone of voice? Task her with developing custom GPTs for different client voices. That meticulous art director? Ask him to establish best practices for using *sref* codes in Midjourney. The magic happens when these responsibilities feel like an extension of someone's professional identity rather than an extra burden. Make this ownership concrete by embedding AI tasks directly into your project plans and timelines. When your team sees tasks like 'Generate initial concept variations with Midjourney' or 'Develop tone exploration using ChatGPT' alongside traditional tasks in your project management system, it sends a powerful signal: this isn't optional – it's just how we work now.

When you win that next major rebrand project, integrate things you've proven through experiments directly into your core workflow. Your strategist doesn't just analyse competitors – they use AI to systematically extract positioning insights from hundreds of content pieces. Your copywriter doesn't just explore voice options – they use tailored prompts to rapidly generate variations for client consideration. Your designers don't just create initial concepts – they use image generation to explore dozens of ideas before committing to development directions. The key to making this work is combining clarity about outcomes with flexibility about methods. Be explicit about what you want people to achieve with AI, but give them room to discover the best way to do it on their own.

This distributed ownership creates a flywheel effect. Each person who incorporates AI into their professional identity becomes another centre of expertise, another source of innovation and another advocate for thoughtful adoption. When everyone owns a piece of your AI transformation, it becomes unstoppable.

Creating shared moments

Culture isn't formed through policies or mission statements – it's built through shared experiences. I've watched agencies struggle with AI adoption until they created what one creative director called 'moments of collective revelation', where teams could see, experience and celebrate AI's impact together.

Institute regular show-and-tell sessions where people demonstrate actual client work enhanced by AI. Keep these ruthlessly practical – no theoretical demonstrations allowed. When a strategist shows how they used AI to analyse 500 customer interviews in an afternoon and extract insights that would have taken days to compile manually, the value becomes undeniable to everyone in the room. One agency we work with instituted a monthly 'AI Lab' – a thirty-minute slot where different departments demonstrate real client work enhanced by AI. The first session featured two tentative examples. By the third month, they needed to extend the meeting to accommodate all the case studies people wanted to share.

The power of these sessions lies in their contagious enthusiasm. When a junior strategist demonstrates how she used AI to analyse five years of customer feedback in three hours – a task that previously took days – her colleagues don't just learn a new technique; they experience a visceral 'I want that, too' moment that no formal training could ever create. Design these showcases to generate friendly competition. A digital agency in Manchester assigns each department a month to showcase their AI applications. 'Nobody wants to be the team with nothing impressive to share,' their MD told me. 'It's created this brilliant creative tension where everyone's constantly looking for new ways to apply these tools.' Don't underestimate the power of public recognition. When your CEO highlights a team that used AI to deliver something that blew the client away, you're not just celebrating those individuals, you're signalling to everyone what success looks like in your evolving culture.

The most valuable outcome isn't just knowledge transfer. It's the shared sense of momentum – the collective feeling that 'we're figuring this out together'. This shared journey transforms AI from something potentially threatening or overwhelming into a team adventure. The investment is minimal, but the cultural return is enormous.

Address specific fears with specific responses

Let's address the elephant in the creative studio: fear. Not just fear of job displacement, but fear of losing creative identity, of becoming dependent on machines, of producing work that feels inauthentic. These aren't irrational concerns. They're legitimate questions about professional purpose and creative integrity. Dismissing them with platitudes about 'AI as a tool' won't work. You need honest conversations about what's changing and what remains fundamentally human. Start by acknowledging the discomfort directly. Don't minimise their feelings. Then reframe the conversation around creative judgement – the uniquely human ability to recognise which AI-generated option will resonate with specific audiences in particular contexts.

Here are some of the more common fears people express:

- **'AI will replace me.'** Response: AI will replace people who refuse to adapt. The creative who masters these tools will be far more valuable than one who ignores them.

- **'Using AI feels like cheating.'** Response: Is using Photoshop cheating? Is spell-check cheating? Tools evolve. Mastery means knowing when and how to use them effectively.

- **'The work won't be authentically mine.'** Response: Your judgement, your taste, your understanding of the brief – that's what makes work yours. AI is like having an infinitely patient intern who can execute your vision quickly.

- **'I don't want to learn new tools constantly.'** Response: Fair enough. But your competitors are learning them. In six months, will clients choose the agency that explores five creative territories or the one that explores fifty?

The breakthrough happens when people stop seeing AI as a threat to their creativity and start seeing it as an amplifier of their existing talents.

Integrating AI into development and recruitment

You don't want to only change how you work today – you also want to systematically build the capabilities you'll need tomorrow. If you're serious about sustained AI advantage, you need to weave it into the very fabric of how you develop and recruit talent.

One of our partners is a recruitment agency specifically for the creative industries. We recently discussed how job descriptions vary across agencies. The difference was striking. The traditional ones listed the usual required skills – Adobe Creative Suite, presentation abilities, strategic thinking. The forward-thinking agencies had already embedded AI literacy alongside these traditional requirements. One creative role specified 'experience using AI tools for prototyping' as a core skill, right next to design expertise.

Start by updating your performance frameworks to reflect this new reality. This doesn't mean expecting everyone to become AI experts overnight, but it does mean establishing AI fluency as a standard professional skill – just as fundamental as using PowerPoint and Google Slides or understanding social media. The key is specificity – generic 'AI skills' mean nothing. Define exactly what capabilities matter for each position. For junior designers, this might mean proficiency with image generation tools for concept exploration. For senior strategists, it could include using language models to synthesise research and identify insights. For client leads, it might focus on AI-assisted briefing and presentation development.

When recruiting, focus on learning agility over specific tool knowledge. The tools are going to change, the aptitude required to adopt them will not. Transform your interview process to evaluate AI readiness. One creative director I work with now includes a scenario-based question: 'Imagine we need to develop five different visual directions for a new beauty brand in forty-eight hours. How might you approach this?' The responses reveal volumes about candidates' AI mindset, not just their technical knowledge.

Investing in AI skills and knowledge

Unlike virtually every technological revolution that came before, AI has a remarkably low barrier to entry. You don't need to learn coding, understand complex systems or master technical jargon. If you can type a question, you can use AI. This accessibility is revolutionary. Think back to the early 2000s, when building even a basic website required specialised knowledge that took months to acquire. Today, your most technologically cautious team member can be up and running with ChatGPT in an afternoon. Don't be fooled by this simplicity, though. The difference between basic usage and transformative application is enormous. I recently heard a CMO talk about two agencies pitching for the same global beauty brand. Both talked about how they would use AI tools in their process. One emphasised how they could deliver the work faster. The other reimagined the entire campaign approach, exploring ideas the CMO hadn't considered possible within their timeline and budget. They won the business by transforming capabilities rather than merely accelerating existing processes.

The most forward-thinking agencies are creating structured learning pathways, recognising that what seems optional today will be what it takes to stay in the game tomorrow. OMG UK has launched an extensive AI training programme that goes far beyond superficial tool introductions. They're methodically transforming their entire organisation of 1,800 employees into what they call 'a fully AI-fluent organisation' through a phased, comprehensive approach. Their Phase 1 training – which they rolled out in April 2025 – includes seven hours of foundational content, covering everything from AI basics to practical applications. They're not just teaching technical skills; they're addressing ethical considerations and legal issues, and developing clear usage policies that provide guardrails for responsible implementation.

What's particularly telling is how they're framing this initiative. OMG's Head of Generative AI, Sean Betts, positions this as preparation for what he calls 'Web 4.0' – a fundamental shift where AI agents will transform our relationship with technology even more profoundly than the digital revolution did two decades ago. This isn't hyperbole from a fringe enthusiast; this is one of the world's largest agency networks making a substantial investment based on their conviction that AI is 'already transforming our industry even faster than the digital revolution did twenty years ago'. Throughout 2025, they're rolling out three additional training phases that progressively deepen their teams' capabilities – covering specific ethical issues like bias and environmental impact, sharing case studies and best practices, and preparing for AI's future role in marketing. Each phase builds on the previous one, creating a comprehensive development journey across the organisation.

The philosophy behind their approach is particularly insightful. As Betts puts it in a LinkedIn post: 'The question isn't "if" we should embrace AI anymore; it's "how well" we implement it.'[34] It's the first time we've seen something like our own AI Accelerator programme developed in-house by an agency. Think about it this way: for decades, we've accepted that mastering design software takes deliberate practice and development. Why would we expect these new, powerful tools to be any different? They're simpler to start with, certainly, but mastery still requires intentional effort.

Morten Legarth at Faith told me:

> 'The number one thing to achieving mastery is just to go and get stuck in. It's a bit like how to run a business – you're not going to learn it by reading a book, you need to just go and do it. It's learn by experience and that's something I really advocate with clients as well.'

Building AI skills relies on three principles that any agency can adopt:

- First, make learning role-specific and immediately applicable. A junior copywriter doesn't need the same

AI skills as a senior strategist. Designers focus on visual prompting techniques while researchers master data synthesis. Each person learns precisely what will enhance their specific responsibilities.

- Second, build learning around real work, not theoretical exercises. When your social media team needs to create content for a well-known client, don't just do it the old way – use it as an opportunity to master AI-assisted content generation, with a senior team member guiding the process.

- Third, create a virtuous cycle of knowledge sharing. Everyone who masters a technique becomes responsible for teaching others, creating an exponential growth in capability that no formal training program can match.

The most forward-thinking agencies are already creating dedicated AI development pathways – structured programs that take people from basic literacy to advanced application in specific domains. One agency in Leeds we've worked with set everyone thirty-, sixty- and ninety-day learning goals. These aren't just training sessions; they're comprehensive journeys that combine learning, application and recognition as people progress. How are you going to build an AI-fluent workforce? The agencies that are thriving in this new landscape share a common trait: they've stopped thinking of AI as something separate that requires extra time, and started seeing it as something that creates time.

Let me share one approach that consistently delivers results. Start by identifying a significant client project coming up in the next month. Block three hours for the team to experiment with relevant AI applications before traditional production work begins. Don't treat this as optional – make it as mandatory as your kick-off meeting. The ROI will be immediately apparent when you see how this investment transforms both the process and the output.

Create a custom AI skills matrix

Here's a practical exercise: get ChatGPT to help you develop a tailored skills matrix for your team using a prompt like this:

> I want to map the most relevant AI skills and tasks for each key role in my agency. Ask me three questions about my agency, one at a time. Then, please list five practical AI skills or capabilities that are especially useful for each role, such as Strategist, Designer, Copywriter, Client Services Manager, New Business Manager.
>
> For each role, include:
>
> - The specific AI use cases or activities they should focus on
>
> - Any mindset or skill shift they may need to adopt
>
> Keep the suggestions practical, role-relevant and based on tasks that are typical in creative agencies.

Training formats that actually work

Watching YouTube tutorials and self-study online courses rarely translates to meaningful change in how teams actually work. It's exactly why, at Spark, we deliver all our training face to face. The right format doesn't just transfer knowledge – it transforms behaviour. Want to create training that actually sticks? Here's how you can implement three approaches that consistently deliver results.

First, replace generic tutorials with workshop-style sessions centred on real client challenges. Block out two hours on a Friday afternoon. Use a current brief you're working on – something with real-world complexity and meaningful stakes. Pair people up and give them an hour to use AI to help them solve part of the problem. Use the second hour to get teams to present back what they learned. This approach connects AI skills directly to daily work, answering the critical question: 'How does this help me solve problems I actually face?' When someone discovers how a tool can shave hours off a tedious research task or expand their creative exploration, you don't need to sell the value – it becomes self-evident.

Second, create pressure-free retrospectives by revisiting completed projects. Select a campaign or deliverable from three to six months ago that went well but presented challenges. Set up a half-day session with this brief: 'How would we approach this differently with the tools we have today?' This method is powerful because there's no deadline pressure inhibiting experimentation, and you already know what a good outcome looks like. The psychological safety this creates is essential for meaningful skill development. Your retrospective sessions should include clear structure: analyse the original process, identify pain points or limitations, apply specific AI techniques to those challenges, and document the new workflow for future projects. These sessions often reveal opportunities that become templates for transforming similar work in the future.

Third, transform individual online learning into collaborative experiences. If team members need to complete specific tutorials, don't send them off separately with links. Instead, schedule a room for ninety minutes, watch key segments together, then immediately apply the techniques to a relevant task. This approach leverages social learning – people retain more when they share with colleagues working through the same challenges. For your design team, this might mean watching a tutorial on structured image prompting, then breaking into pairs to apply those techniques to a current visual challenge. For your strategy team, it could involve learning research synthesis methods, then collaboratively using them to analyse a dataset you're currently working with. To accelerate progression, create clear expectations for application after each training session: 'By next week's team meeting, everyone should have used this technique on at least one task and be ready to share their experience'. This accountability transforms learning from theoretical to practical in the critical early phase when habits are forming.

What sets successful agency training apart isn't fancy technology or complex methodologies – it's always staying relevant. Every minute spent learning must connect directly to the work your team actually does, solving problems they actually face, within the constraints under which they actually operate. Achieve that, and you'll not only create new skills, but fundamental changes in how your agency delivers value.

Creating AI learning journeys

Imagine a copywriter joining your team today. Without a structured journey, their development will be random – picking up tips from colleagues, watching occasional tutorials, perhaps experimenting, when deadlines allow. However, with a clear learning pathway, they know exactly how to progress from basic competence to genuine expertise.

Here's what an effective copywriter's journey might look like:

At the **Foundation level**, they master the essentials: understanding how AI writing tools work, crafting basic prompts for different content types and developing the important skill of critically reviewing and editing AI-generated text. Their first milestone challenge might be creating initial drafts for three different client deliverables using AI assistance.

Once comfortable with the basics, they progress to the **Intermediate level**, where they learn advanced prompt techniques for controlling tone and style precisely. They develop methods for rapidly exploring multiple creative directions, and, critically, learn to blend AI capabilities with their own creative judgement. Their showcase project at this level might be developing a complete content package for a client using an AI-augmented workflow.

At the **Advanced level**, they begin creating custom solutions: building specialised writing assistants for specific clients or industries, developing reusable prompt frameworks that ensure consistent results across projects, and taking on responsibility for helping others develop their skills. Their capstone challenge becomes designing a comprehensive AI-augmented process for complex content projects.

The power of structured journeys extends to every role in your agency. For designers, the progression might move from basic image generation to advanced visual exploration techniques, to developing custom visual styles for client brands. For strategists, it might advance from automated research synthesis to insight generation to developing proprietary AI-enhanced strategic frameworks.

The crucial element isn't just the content of these pathways – it's how they integrate with your broader talent development approach. Make AI capability development an explicit part of performance discussions: 'To progress to Senior Copywriter, we expect you to demonstrate intermediate AI skills in client work'. Connect milestones on their journey to practical client challenges: 'This project for our healthcare client is an opportunity to apply those advanced prompt techniques you've been developing'.

One agency we work with has integrated their AI learning journeys directly into their professional development framework. As their MD explained: 'We've made it clear that advancing your AI capabilities isn't optional or separate from your core skills development – it's an integral part of growing in your role.' Don't leave your team's AI development to chance. Map the journey, provide the resources, celebrate the milestones and watch capabilities transform from basic to extraordinary across your entire agency.

Want to create a role-specific learning programme quickly? Try this prompt:

> Create a one-week AI learning programme for [ROLE] at my creative agency. Design five daily lessons (Mon–Fri) that build on each other, with each lesson taking no more than fifteen minutes to complete.
>
> The programme should focus on [SPECIFIC USE CASE] and result in a tangible deliverable by Friday that could be used in a real client project.
>
> For each day, include:
>
> 1. A clear learning objective
> 2. A brief explanation of the concept (300–500 words)
> 3. A step-by-step task using AI tools
> 4. A specific prompt to run in [AI TOOL]
> 5. A reflection question to reinforce learning
>
> Structure the overall week to progress from basic to more advanced applications, assuming the person has limited time but is motivated to learn.

Making it stick: Beyond the initial enthusiasm

The biggest risk to your AI transformation isn't resistance – it's the inevitable plateau that occurs after the initial enthusiasm wanes. People try the tools, see some benefits, then gradually revert to familiar methods when deadlines approach and the pressure mounts. Prevent this backslide by embedding AI applications into standard operating procedures, not treating them as optional extras. When AI-enhanced research becomes part of your strategy development process, when visual exploration using image generation becomes standard creative practice, when AI-assisted project planning becomes the norm, that's when transformation becomes permanent:

- Include AI exploration phases in project timelines.
- Add AI application checkpoints to quality control processes.
- Reference AI-enhanced capabilities in client service agreements.
- Make AI tools accessible within existing creative software workflows.

The goal isn't to become an 'AI agency' – it's to become an agency that uses every available tool to deliver exceptional results for your clients. AI should become the invisible infrastructure that enhances everything you do, not a special feature you occasionally deploy.

Key takeaways

- **Leadership drives adoption.** Agencies succeeding with AI have visible commitment from the top, with senior leaders actively participating in and championing the journey.

- **Structure creates momentum.** A well-defined AI taskforce with clear responsibilities, protected time and actual authority speeds up adoption far more effectively than grassroots enthusiasm alone.

- **Cultural transformation happens by design.** AI-forward cultures don't emerge accidentally; they're built through deliberate experiences, shared moments and recognition systems that celebrate experimentation.

- **AI literacy becomes a core professional skill.** Just as proficiency in Adobe Creative Suite became non-negotiable, AI competence is rapidly becoming essential for career progression in creative industries.

- **Resistance reveals legitimate concerns.** Scepticism often stems from valid questions about professional identity and creative authenticity, requiring thoughtful responses rather than dismissive reassurance.

- **Role-specific training beats generic workshops.** Copywriters need different AI skills than strategists, who need different capabilities than designers – tailor professional development to actual job requirements.

- **Learning must be applied.** Theoretical AI knowledge without immediate application is quickly forgotten; build all training around actual client work and real challenges your agency faces.

- **Progress requires progression.** Clear learning journeys with defined milestones transform vague aspirations into measurable development, preventing the common plateau effect.

Your action point: Launch the transformation

Block out two hours next month for your entire team. Divide them into pairs that mix AI confidence levels with complementary skills. Give each pair this specific challenge: 'Take a client project from the last three months and explore how AI could have enhanced one aspect of your work – research, ideation, visual exploration or client presentation'. Document what each pair discovers: one technique that worked and one approach that didn't deliver expected results. This single session will reveal your agency's AI readiness, identify natural champions and create momentum for systematic adoption. Most importantly, it transforms AI from an abstract possibility to a practical reality that is grounded in actual client work.

11
Data and tools

What if every email exchange about a client's business challenge contains the seeds of your next strategic insight? What if every recorded client call holds patterns of decision making that could transform your pitching process? What if the brand guidelines you created three years ago could inform a new campaign today?

In the AI era, everything is now data – and the agencies that understand this shift are pulling ahead of those still treating their information as mere by-products of the creative process. We're used to thinking of data as stuff that sits in spreadsheets and databases. The things that machines can read. However, LLMs can read almost anything: the email thread where you discussed the brief with your client, the conversation you had with your creative director about how to approach the project, the assets you created for their campaign last year. However, having valuable data isn't enough on its own. You need clear, structured workflows that embed AI into your everyday processes. These workflows distinguish between the sporadic, personality-driven AI experiments happening across the industry and the consistent, business-wide adoption that delivers measurable results for clients.

During our research with thirty creative agency leaders, two consistent themes emerged: agencies that had successfully integrated AI had both rethought their approach to data and implemented workflows that blended human expertise with AI capabilities, playing to the strengths of both.

In this chapter, we'll explore:

- Why everything your agency produces should now be considered potential AI training data
- Practical approaches to organising your data for maximum AI accessibility
- A step-by-step approach to embedding AI into your agency workflows
- How to balance automation and human oversight for optimal results

The transition starts with a simple but profound shift in mindset: your agency doesn't just create campaigns or designs – it creates data, and that data, properly harnessed, could be your most powerful strategic asset.

Everything is now data

Most agency leaders stare blankly when you mention 'data strategy'. It sounds technical, complex and far removed from the creative work they love. However, what many don't realise is that they're already sitting on a wealth of information that could transform their business – if only they knew how to use it.

Think of structured data as information that fits neatly into tables and spreadsheets – client contact details, project timelines, campaign metrics and financial records. It's organised, searchable and easily understood by computers. However, 80% or more of your agency's data isn't structured at all. This 'dark data' – your meeting transcripts, client emails, creative briefs, brand guidelines, presentations, research interviews, social media content and even sketches and mood boards – contains immense value that traditional systems simply couldn't access. Now, LLMs can read all of this information and make sense of it. In practical terms, this means your agency can now:

- Extract insights from years of client conversations
- Identify patterns across dozens of creative briefs to spot recurring client challenges
- Use transcripts of client calls and team brainstorms to draft creative briefs
- Look again at forgotten strategic approaches from past projects that could be relevant today
- Analyse sentiments across client communications to gauge satisfaction and identify issues
- Convert hand-drawn concepts into digital assets that can be refined and developed

Kate Ross at eight&four told me:

'We're directly embedding data from our different performance platforms and use natural language to query the data. That's been interesting because it's moving away from that model of monthly reports for the client and instead now it's just an always on feature, and they can just interact with that data using natural language questions.'

This is what happens when you make your data work for you.

Making your data work for you

You've done the training, bought licences to all the latest AI tools, and you're ready to go. There's just one small problem: your beautiful creative work is locked away in formats that AI can't read, your filenames look like a Wi-Fi passcode, key decisions are buried in email threads and handwritten notes, and finding anything useful feels like archaeological detective work. This isn't about building some complex technical infrastructure that requires a computer science degree; it's about getting organised in a way that actually helps you work smarter. Think of it like this: you've just hired a brilliant new designer who's talented, eager and ready to dive in. However, when they show up on Monday morning, ready to get stuck into that client rebrand, they don't know where to start. 'Where's the brief?' they ask. 'What's the client like? What's their brand about? What did the last campaign we ran for them look like? What worked? What didn't?' You realise it's going to take you half an hour to dig out the documents. Your brilliant designer can't get started – not because they lack talent, but because you haven't given them the information to succeed. This is exactly what happens when you try to work with AI tools.

The intern test

Here's a simple way to think about organising your data: could a bright intern walk into your agency tomorrow and quickly get up to speed on your projects? If the answer is no, your AI tools will struggle too. Let's work backwards from what that intern actually needs to be helpful. They need to find things quickly, without spending half their day hunting for brand guidelines or trying to decode mysterious filenames. They need context about the client. Who are we working for? What do they care about What's their history with the agency? What's worked for them before? They need to understand the project itself. What are we trying to achieve? What constraints are we working within? What's the creative brief actually asking for? Most importantly, they need access to the thinking behind the work. Why did the team make certain decisions? What client feedback shaped the direction? What alternatives were considered and rejected? Finally, they need examples of good work. What does success look like for this client? What framework does your agency use to build campaign strategy? How do they like to communicate? If you can't quickly provide this information to an intern, you won't be able to provide it to AI either. The same organisational principles that help new team members get up to speed will transform how effectively your AI tools can contribute to client work. Let's run through what this looks like in practice, using that rebrand project as an example.

How to structure your data for AI

Step 1: Make everything findable

Your intern shouldn't need a treasure map to find basic information about your projects. I know this seems painfully obvious, but I've watched a creative director spend ten minutes hunting for a document while we were on a video call together, and when he found it, the file name was something that looked like a military cipher. When you're prompting an AI tool, being able to say 'use the Nationwide brand guidelines' instead of 'Um, it's that file that starts with PRJ something' makes all the difference. Your AI assistant can't guess what's in mystery files or folders any better than your intern can.

Step 2: Create the AI briefing folder

For each client, create what I call a 'briefing folder'. It contains everything an intern (or AI) would need to understand the work. Think about what you'd hand to someone on their first day:

- The client brief and strategy documents (so they understand the mission)

- Brand guidelines and tone of voice (so they can speak like the client)

- Meeting transcripts and key emails (where the real insights live)

- Research findings and audience insights (the thinking behind the thinking)

- Examples of previous work (what 'good' looks like for this client)
- Project timeline and budget (the constraints they're working within)

Step 3: Document the decisions

Your intern needs to understand not just what you delivered, but why you made certain choices. This is where most agencies fall down. When your team decides to reject a creative concept, capture the reasoning: 'Too similar to Competitor X's latest campaign', or 'Brilliant idea but would blow the production budget', or 'Doesn't ladder up to our brand positioning'. When a client gives feedback that changes direction, save that conversation. When your producer finds a clever solution to a technical challenge, document it. This isn't bureaucracy – it's building institutional memory. The next task you work on (human or AI) can learn from decisions that would otherwise be lost.

Step 4: Make creative work visible

Here's where the intern analogy gets interesting. You could show an intern your Photoshop file and they'd see your creative work, but AI tools can't see inside proprietary formats. Your layered PSD files, your Illustrator artwork, your InDesign layouts – to AI, they might as well not exist. You need to export flattened versions:

- Save design files as JPEGs or PNGs alongside your working files.
- Export presentations as PDFs as well as native formats.

- Render videos to MP4s alongside your Premiere project files.
- Save copy as plain text or a PDF in addition to Word or Google docs.

At Spark, we create an 'AI Assets' folder for every project. When we finish a creative milestone, we export everything to universal formats. It takes a few extra minutes, but it means our AI tools can actually see what we've created.

Collecting the data you need

Here's something most agencies miss entirely: your most valuable insights often come from conversations that never get documented. Your intern would benefit enormously from listening to client calls, sitting in on brainstorms, understanding how decisions get made in real time, but unless you're recording and transcribing these conversations, they're lost forever. Most video conferencing platforms now transcribe automatically. These transcripts become searchable archives of your team's and your client's thinking, strategic insights and creative reasoning. Your AI tools can analyse these conversations to spot patterns: 'This client always requests changes to tone of voice at the first review' or 'They're typically cautious and need extra time for legal approval'.

The privacy briefing

Of course, you wouldn't give an intern access to everything on day one. You'd explain what they can see, what requires approval and what's absolutely confidential. The same principle applies to AI tools. Establish clear guidelines for your team,:

- What data can be used with which AI tools
- Who has permission to access different types of information
- What requires anonymising before AI analysis
- Which tools can you trust with sensitive client data

One agency I know colour-codes their folders: green for 'AI-friendly', amber for 'internal use only', and red for 'absolutely confidential'. A simple system, but it prevents accidentally feeding client financial data into a public AI tool.

The five-minute intern test

If this all sounds overwhelming, try the five-minute intern test. At the end of each project, spend five minutes asking: 'Could someone new understand this work quickly?' It's like leaving notes for the next person who has to pick up where you left off – except that next person might be an AI tool. Your brilliant intern needs context, clear information and well-organised files to do great work. Your AI tools need exactly the same things.

Connecting AI to your digital workspace

The integration between AI systems and workspace tools is transforming rapidly. There are three developments worth noting:

1. **Google Workspace integration:** Google has begun to embed Gemini deeply into Workspace, making it an

extension of tools you likely already use. This means your Docs, Sheets, Slides and Drive content are now seamlessly connected to AI capabilities. For agencies using Google Workspace, this creates a natural environment where AI can access your content without requiring many manual uploads or complex integrations.

2. **Microsoft Copilot integration:** Likewise, if your agency runs on Microsoft 365, Copilot offers powerful integration across the Office ecosystem. Copilot lives inside Word, Excel, PowerPoint, Teams, SharePoint and Outlook, giving you AI assistance exactly where you're already working. It can pull insights from multiple documents across your SharePoint. For agencies already invested in the Microsoft ecosystem, Copilot can eliminate the friction of switching between tools and manually feeding information to AI systems.

3. **ChatGPT connectors:** Similarly, ChatGPT now offers the ability to connect directly to your Google Drive, creating a powerful bridge between your existing data and sophisticated AI capabilities. This means you can prompt ChatGPT to analyse specific documents, presentations or datasets that exist in your drive without having to manually copy content.

The key advantage of these integrated approaches is that they meet you where you already work, rather than requiring you to learn entirely new systems or completely restructure how your team collaborates. These integrations are eliminating friction points between your data and AI tools, but they also require thoughtful governance. Every agency should establish clear policies about:

- Which workspace tools can connect to which AI services
- What permissions these connections should have
- How to ensure client confidentiality when using these integrations
- Who can establish new connections between systems

As these integrations continue to evolve, the line between your workspace and AI tools will blur further, making data management both simpler and more consequential.

Starting small: A practical approach

This might all sound overwhelming, but the key is to start small. Don't try to reorganise your entire data archive overnight.

Instead:

1. Begin with new projects going forward.
2. Implement AI-friendly practices from day one.
3. Create a template for your AI training folders.
4. Gradually extend these practices to your most active clients.
5. Set aside time to periodically retroactively organise high-value historical data.

Remember, the goal isn't perfection – it's progress. Even small improvements in how you manage your data can yield significant benefits when working with AI tools.

Embedding AI into your workflows

Understanding that everything is data is only half the equation. The other half is turning AI from a novelty into part of your agency's operational DNA. Right now, your AI use probably looks like this: Sarah uses ChatGPT for brainstorming, Tom uses it to re-draft emails, and your strategy team asks AI to summarise research reports. Your AI adoption looks like a teenager's bedroom. Scattered, inconsistent and entirely dependent on individual enthusiasm. What happens when your most AI-savvy team member goes on holiday? What happens when a client asks how you're using AI in their project? What happens when you're pitching against an agency that's actually integrated AI into their workflow? What you need are AI-augmented workflows, documented processes that show exactly where AI enhances your work and where humans remain in control. Think about it: you wouldn't let your team wing it when it comes to client onboarding or creative development. You have processes, templates, quality checks. Your AI adoption needs the same rigour.

Most agencies treat AI like a Swiss Army Knife – a handy tool you reach for when you need it, but one everybody uses differently. However, AI works best when it's woven into the fabric of how you work. The difference? Successful agencies have stopped thinking about AI as a neat tool and started integrating it as a team member. They're asking: where should our AI assistant sit in this process? What should it handle? What should humans keep control of? What you need is a systematic approach to embedding AI into your workflows. Not some complicated consultancy framework, but a simple five-step method you can apply to any process in your agency.

Step 1: Document what should happen

This isn't about capturing your current messy reality – it's about designing the optimal process. For example, let's think about what client onboarding should look like if you could start afresh tomorrow. Map out the ideal activities for bringing a new client on board:

1. **Client briefing session:** Have a comprehensive discussion with the client to understand their requirements and objectives.

2. **Internal team alignment:** Brief your internal team and establish a shared understanding of the opportunity.

3. **Planning, budgeting and resourcing:** Develop a detailed project plan with realistic timelines and resource allocation.

4. **Dig into the brief and find what's missing:** Analyse the initial brief to identify gaps and areas that need clarification, then research and gather additional context to get a comprehensive understanding.

5. **Get client sign-off on the final brief, plan and budget:** Present a complete project framework and secure a formal agreement.

Design this process based on what would deliver the best outcomes for your clients, not based on what you're currently constrained by. You're building the ideal workflow that AI will help you achieve.

Step 2: Break each activity into key tasks

Now, take each ideal activity and identify the three to five main tasks that would make it excellent. Think about what needs to happen to deliver outstanding results.

Take the activity 'Dig into the brief and find what's missing':

- Systematically review the initial brief against comprehensive project criteria.
- Highlight areas where the client's objectives need further clarification.
- Research the client's industry landscape and competitive environment.
- Identify gaps in the target audience's understanding and the market context.
- Flag any missing technical specifications or deliverable requirements.
- Collect relevant case studies and examples of successful approaches.

You're designing for excellence, not efficiency. AI will help you achieve both.

Step 3: Identify the data each activity needs

For each activity in your ideal workflow, ask what information an assistant would need to do this brilliantly.

For 'Dig into the brief and find what's missing', you'll need:

- The initial client brief and any supporting materials
- A comprehensive template or checklist of the brief's requirements
- Examples of well-developed briefs from similar projects
- Access to market research and industry reports

This step helps you understand not just what data you need, but what data would unlock truly exceptional work.

Step 4: Decide who takes the lead

Here's where strategy meets reality. For each activity, decide whether AI should handle the heavy lifting with human oversight, or whether humans should lead with AI providing powerful assistance. Activities that involve processing large amounts of information or systematic analysis should be AI first, with a human overseeing and reviewing the outputs. 'Research the client's industry landscape' should probably be AI first, with a human reviewing the AI's findings and adding strategic interpretation. Meanwhile, activities that require relationship building, creative thinking or nuanced judgement should probably be human first, with an AI assistant to help bounce ideas around and sharpen your thinking. 'Client briefing session' should probably be human first, but using AI to help prepare for the meeting and generate the follow up email. The goal is to amplify human capabilities, not replace human judgement.

Step 5: Pick the right tool for each job

Next you need to select the minimum number of AI tools that will help you achieve your ideal process, but how do you evaluate which tools deserve a place in your agency's stack?

Consider whether you need a good prompt into a standard AI tool like ChatGPT or Claude, or whether your specific requirements justify building a custom GPT or even a specialist platform. A generic language model might handle most copywriting tasks brilliantly, but a fashion brand might benefit from custom image-generation models trained on their aesthetic. The key is matching the tool's sophistication to the task's complexity – don't overcomplicate simple needs or under-resource complex ones. Evaluate how tools support collaboration across your team. The most powerful AI implementations happen when multiple people can contribute to and benefit from the same system. Can your strategist share the AI notebook they've been working on with their project team? Does your chosen tool allow you to share prompt libraries and collaboratively refine your ideas?

Pay close attention to workflow integration. Tools that connect seamlessly with your existing systems – Google Workspace, Microsoft SharePoint, Adobe Creative Suite, project management platforms – reduce friction and increase adoption. ChatGPT now integrates with HubSpot, for example. The best AI tool in the world becomes useless if your team avoids it because it's too complicated to access. Next, think about data privacy. Where does your information live? What controls does the platform provide? Who has access to your inputs and outputs? These questions become critical when handling client data, and the wrong choice here can derail relationships and create legal complications. Then, consider cost in the context of value delivered. A £30 monthly ChatGPT subscription that saves your team ten hours weekly represents extraordinary value. However, a £500 monthly specialist platform that marginally improves one workflow probably doesn't. The goal is building sustainable capability, not impressive technology for its own sake.

Finally, walk before you run. Almost everything you can achieve with AI can be done with a meeting notetaker, an LLM with custom GPTs or the equivalent, and a diffusion (image) model. Don't overcomplicate things.

Building your prompt library: The knowledge multiplier

One of the most effective ways to scale AI expertise across your agency is through a well-curated prompt library – a shared repository of proven techniques that transforms every individual's discoveries into collective capabilities. Start by choosing a platform where your team naturally goes to find resources, whether that's a shared Google Doc, a dedicated Slack channel or a section in your project management system. The key is meeting people where they already work rather than creating another place they need to remember to check.

Organise your prompts into logical categories that mirror how people actually think about their work – research and analysis, creative development, client communication, project management. This isn't about perfect taxonomy; it's about helping someone find what they need in under thirty seconds. Begin collecting prompts that are already delivering results for your team members, starting small with perhaps ten proven examples rather than trying to anticipate every possible scenario.

Document each prompt thoroughly, with its purpose, practical examples of successful outputs, tips for optimal results, and clear instructions for customisation using placeholders like [CLIENT NAME] or [PROJECT TYPE]. This context transforms a simple text string into a reusable framework that others can adapt confidently. Appoint a curator – or one for each department – to manage submissions, maintain quality standards and keep the library current as tools evolve and new techniques emerge.

Most importantly, make your prompt library a living resource by regularly sharing updates and improvements in team meetings or through dedicated channels. When someone discovers a breakthrough technique or refines an existing prompt, that knowledge should flow immediately to everyone who could benefit. This systematic approach to knowledge sharing accelerates learning, prevents people from repeatedly solving the same problems, and ensures your agency's AI capabilities grow collectively rather than remaining trapped in individual silos.

Key takeaways

- **Everything is now data.** Your meeting transcripts, email threads, brand guidelines and creative briefs become powerful AI training materials that transform generic tools into informed collaborators. LLMs can now read and understand unstructured information like client conversations and strategy documents that traditional systems couldn't process.

- **The 'intern test' reveals AI readiness.** If a bright new hire couldn't quickly understand your projects and clients from your current file organisation, neither can your AI tools.

- **AI-friendly data organisation requires human-readable systems.** Clear file naming, consistent folder structures and exported assets in universal formats dramatically improve AI performance.

- **Workflow integration beats tool proliferation.** Systematically embedding AI into existing processes using the five-step method creates sustainable change rather than scattered experiments.

- **Document your ideal process first.** Design what excellent client work should look like, then map where AI enhances human capabilities rather than trying to automate existing inefficiencies.

- **Workspace integrations eliminate friction.** Google Workspace, Microsoft Copilot and ChatGPT connections create seamless bridges between your existing data and AI capabilities.

- **Prompt libraries scale institutional knowledge.** Building collections of proven prompts and custom GPTs makes individual discoveries available to everyone, accelerating team-wide adoption.

Your action point: Run the five-minute intern test

Pick your most recent completed project and spend five minutes assessing its AI readiness. Could someone new to your agency quickly understand the client, the brief, the creative direction and the reasoning behind key decisions from your current files and folders? Create a simple 'briefing pack' containing the essential context an intern (or AI) would need: clearly named files, a project summary explaining what happened and why, and key assets exported to universal formats. This exercise reveals gaps in your data organisation while creating a template you can apply to future projects, making your agency's knowledge systematically accessible to AI tools.

12
Governance and accountability

Have you ever watched a trapeze artist at the circus? When an acrobat launches into seemingly impossible feats high above the ground, it appears effortless – even magical. But look closer. What's that below? A safety net. That safety net is the difference between breath-taking artistry and reckless endangerment. It's what allows the performer to push boundaries and take creative risks. The net doesn't limit their performance, it enables it. In your creative business, AI governance serves exactly the same purpose. As we've explored throughout this book, AI offers many opportunities to transform how creative work happens. It can amplify your team's capabilities, automate mundane tasks and even open entirely new revenue streams. However, without proper guidelines, this powerful technology can become a liability rather than an asset. During my research for this book, I spoke with dozens of agency leaders about their AI journey. One creative director told me: 'We had a client question us about data privacy and copyright that we couldn't properly answer. We looked really unprofessional.'

This chapter is your safety net. We'll examine how to establish practical governance frameworks that protect your business without stifling innovation. We'll explore how to craft sensible AI policies, ensure transparency for your clients and create accountability systems that keep your AI initiatives on track. This isn't about creating bureaucracy or red tape. It's about giving your team the confidence to experiment boldly within clear boundaries. It's about demonstrating to clients that you're thoughtful and responsible in how you deploy these powerful tools. Ultimately, it's about ensuring your AI adoption journey delivers sustainable value rather than trips you up with unexpected hazards.

Governance: What's important to your clients

Proper governance becomes particularly critical when navigating today's diverse client landscape. You'll increasingly find yourself caught between two opposing client perspectives – sometimes within the same organisation.

On one side, there are clients who view AI with deep suspicion. Most commonly they belong to heavily regulated industries like financial services or healthcare, or they've been burned by negative press about AI. They'll ask pointed questions: Will you be using AI with my data? How do you ensure compliance? What about copyright issues? Without a robust governance framework, these conversations quickly become uncomfortable. A strategy director at a London agency shared this insight:

> 'We developed a one-page AI policy statement specifically for our compliance-focused clients. It outlines exactly how we use AI, how we use client data, what safeguards we have in place, and the specific tools we employ, and where they store their data. Having this document helps turn those difficult conversations from defensive explanations to confident reassurances.'

We have also had several agencies tell us they have been required to publish their AI governance and data practices to pitch for jobs on government frameworks or large RFP processes. Having this information at your fingertips – or even published on your website – will set you apart. On the opposite end are clients who've read about AI's efficiency gains and expect substantial cost reductions: 'If you're using AI, shouldn't this be cheaper?' They view AI purely as an automation tool that reduces human effort, rather than as a means to enhance quality and explore more creative possibilities. Through our workshops and programmes, we've spoken to a number of agencies who have encountered clients expecting AI to reduce costs. A robust governance framework helps you navigate both scenarios by providing documented evidence of your responsible approach for cautious clients, and clearly articulating where and how AI creates value beyond cost-cutting for your price-focused clients. Let's build that safety net together.

Building an AI policy

I know what you're thinking; 'AI governance framework' sounds about as exciting as watching paint dry. Trust me, I get it. This is the part where many would be tempted to skip ahead – the business equivalent of agreeing to terms and conditions without reading them. This seemingly dull bit is what will save you countless headaches down the road. Think of it as insurance. Nobody gets excited about buying insurance until they need to make a claim. Similarly, nobody gets excited about governance frameworks until a client asks pointed questions about data privacy or an employee inadvertently breaches copyright using AI tools. At its core, an AI policy is simply a document that outlines how your agency uses AI tools. It clarifies what's acceptable, what's not, which tools are approved, how data should be handled, and who's responsible for what. Your policy doesn't need to be a legal masterpiece or hundreds of pages long. It should be clear, accessible and actually useful. Here's what to include:

- **Purpose and scope:** What the policy aims to achieve and who it applies to. Keep this straightforward: 'This policy guides how we use AI tools at [Agency Name] to ensure responsible innovation'.

- **Governance structure:** Who's responsible for overseeing AI usage? Is there an AI taskforce or committee? Who should staff consult if they have questions?

- **Approved AI tools:** A list of vetted and authorised AI platforms and applications, with the logins or usernames each team should use. This prevents employees from using tools you're uncomfortable with or that have questionable data practices.

- **Data privacy and security:** Guidelines for handling sensitive data with AI tools. This section should clearly define what data can and cannot be used with AI tools, particularly concerning clients' information. When should data be anonymised? What about data that includes personal details? What data should be deleted at the end of a project?

- **Transparency and disclosure:** This outlines the principles guiding how you inform your clients about AI usage. When should you disclose AI use? What level of detail is appropriate? What should clients be able to dictate, and what is a standard part of the way you work?

- **Compliance:** How will you know the guidelines have been followed for each client? Outline how project teams will be expected to indicate they have followed the rules and sign off on where AI has been used for client work.

- **Risk assessment and mitigation:** Procedures for identifying and addressing potential AI-related risks. What things might go wrong? And what should people do if it does?

- **Policy ownership and review:** Who is responsible for maintaining the policy and how often it will be reviewed. AI is evolving rapidly, so your policy should, too. Think about revisiting it every three to six months.

Here's where it's easy to go wrong – you create a policy, share it once, then let it gather digital dust in a forgotten folder. To make your policy valuable, you need to treat it as a living document that actively guides decisions every day rather than a compliance exercise that sits on a shelf. Start by storing your policy somewhere everyone can find it easily – not buried in a departmental folder or hidden in your company handbook, but prominently placed where people naturally look for guidance. Make it part of your project management system, link it from your agency intranet, or include it in your standard client onboarding materials. Communication matters far more than creation. Don't just email the policy out and assume everyone will read it. Discuss it in team meetings, reference specific sections when relevant situations arise, and make sure everyone understands why these guidelines matter for protecting both the agency and clients. The policy only works if people remember it exists when they need it most. Keep the language accessible and jargon-free. Your team needs to understand the policy, not just comply with it. Avoid legal terminology or technical explanations that require interpretation. If a junior account manager can't quickly grasp what they should or shouldn't do with client data, your policy needs simplifying. Consider making your policy interactive and searchable. A digital agency in Leeds we've worked with created an AI Policy Chatbot using ChatGPT:

> 'We transformed our AI policy into a conversational Q&A format. Team members can ask questions in plain English and get immediate answers about our guidelines. It's been far more effective than expecting everyone to read and remember a static document.'

Remember that the quest for a perfect policy is the enemy of a producing a good one. Start with something simple but functional, then refine it as your AI usage matures and you encounter real-world scenarios which your initial version didn't anticipate. A basic policy that people actually use beats a comprehensive one that nobody references.

Communicating with clients

The moment has arrived. Your agency has embraced AI tools, developed clear governance frameworks and trained your team.

Now comes perhaps the most delicate part of the journey: explaining your approach to clients. This conversation is a balancing act. Share too little, and clients might worry about what's happening behind the scenes. Share too much technical detail, and their eyes glaze over. Position it poorly, and they might question your fees. Get it right, though, and you transform AI from a potential point of friction into a compelling advantage. Not all clients view AI through the same lens. In my conversations, a clear pattern has emerged. Clients are on their own AI journey, and typically fall somewhere on what I call the 'AI Acceptance Spectrum'. Understanding where your clients sit on this spectrum isn't just about categorising them – it's about recognising their fundamental concerns and addressing them head-on. Here's what's really keeping them up at night, and what you need to do about it.

1. The hard no

'We don't want AI used on our account at all'.

Their core concern is risk and control. They're worried about brand safety, potential legal issues and losing control over their brand narrative, often driven by legal teams or risk-averse leadership who've seen too many AI horror stories in the press.

What you need to do:

- Respect this boundary completely – no exceptions, no shortcuts.

- Build trust by being completely transparent about your AI governance.

- Keep the door open for future conversations by sharing case studies of what you've achieved for other clients.

2. The data guardians

'You can use it internally, but don't put our data into these systems'.

Their core concern is data security and regulatory compliance. They're comfortable with AI in principle, but terrified of data breaches, GDPR violations or sensitive information ending up in training datasets.

What you need to do:

- Explain how your AI policy addresses data privacy and how your team are trained on data handling best practices.
- Show you use enterprise-grade AI tools with proper data protection guarantees.
- Consider on-premise or private cloud AI solutions for the most sensitive accounts.

3. The output sceptics

'Use it for research and ideation, but not for final deliverables'.

Their core concern is quality and authenticity. They worry that AI-generated content will look generic, damage their brand's unique voice, or make them appear to be cutting corners with their audience.

What you need to do:

- Position AI as a creative enhancement tool, not a replacement for human creativity.

- Show your creative process – how AI helps generate better human ideas.
- Maintain rigorous quality control on all outputs with human oversight at every stage.
- Build custom AI tools trained on their brand guidelines and tone of voice.

4. The transparency seekers

'We're comfortable with AI use, but want to know how and where'.

Their core concern is disclosure and education. They want to understand the value AI brings and ensure they can confidently explain their approach to stakeholders, customers or regulators.

What you need to do:

- Develop clear AI usage documentation and reporting.
- Build AI usage into your project reporting and invoicing.
- Help them develop their own AI communication guidelines.

5. The enthusiastic adopters

'Let's push the boundaries of what's possible with this technology'.

Their core concern is competitive advantage and ROI. They want to be ahead of the curve but need to justify investments and demonstrate tangible business benefits.

What you need to do:

- Become their strategic AI partner, not just a service provider.
- Develop custom AI solutions that create competitive moats.
- Stay ahead of the latest AI developments and opportunities.
- Help them communicate their AI leadership to their stakeholders.
- Pilot new AI technologies and tools on their account first.

Remember: clients who start as a hard 'no' can become your biggest AI advocates once they see the quality and professionalism of your approach.

When clients say no

Despite your best efforts, some clients will remain resistant to AI use. Rather than viewing this as an obstacle, treat it as an opportunity to demonstrate your client-centricity and governance maturity. One agency explained to me that:

> 'We have what we call our "Red Client" protocol. For clients who require no AI usage, we have clear workflows and checkpoints to ensure compliance with their preferences. This actually became a selling point – even AI-sceptical clients appreciate that we have thoughtful systems in place.'

The key is developing robust systems that respect clients' boundaries while showcasing your professionalism. Start by creating a simple internal categorisation system that flags clients' AI preferences from the moment they onboard. This might be as straightforward as colour-coding clients' folders or adding clear indicators to project management systems that immediately signal to team members how AI can or cannot be used on specific accounts. Build self-certification into your standard workflows by creating simple checklists that appear in clients' folders or on the front page of a project's documents. Team members can quickly confirm they've complied with a client's AI preferences before any work leaves the agency. This creates accountability without bureaucracy, ensuring compliance becomes second nature rather than an afterthought.

Finally, don't forget to schedule periodic check-ins about AI with reluctant clients as both the technology and their comfort levels evolve. What feels impossible today might become acceptable tomorrow as industry standards shift and regulatory clarity emerges. These conversations position you as a thoughtful partner rather than a pushy vendor, building trust that often leads to more openness over time. One of the most fascinating contradictions I've encountered is what I call the 'AI perception gap' – clients who express strong reservations about AI tools while happily using AI-powered features in existing software. A typical example is the client that's uncomfortable using Midjourney, but thinks Generative Fill feature in Photoshop is a wonderful time saver. This gap stems from several factors:

1. **The invisible integration effect:** When AI is seamlessly integrated into familiar tools, it's perceived as just another feature rather than as 'artificial intelligence'.

2. **Brand trust transfer:** Established brands like Adobe or Google lend legitimacy to AI features that standalone AI tools lack.

3. **Terminology confusion:** Many clients have formed opinions about 'AI' without a clear understanding of what the term encompasses.

This gap in understanding presents both a challenge and an opportunity. The strategic approach is not to correct clients bluntly ('Actually, that's AI too!') but to use their comfort with integrated AI as a bridge to broader acceptance. Start by discussing the AI-powered tools they're already using and enjoying. This creates some common ground before expanding the conversation to other applications. It's typically much more effective than abstract discussions about the technology.

In the current environment of uncertainty around AI, transparency itself becomes a powerful differentiator. Agencies that openly discuss their AI approaches, limitations and governance build significantly stronger client trust. Think about including a simple section in all your proposals called 'How we use AI in this project'.

Sometimes, of course, it's nothing to do with you. Kate Ross at eight&four puts it perfectly:

> 'People are very scared of AI. You show a CMO this amazing AI product, they say "Wow, that's incredible". Then reality hits – what if this means I only need half my team? Some people want big teams, they want their kingdoms, and AI threatens that power.'

The £50,000 question

'If AI makes things faster, shouldn't our fees be lower?' You've heard this question. Probably more than once. If you haven't

GOVERNANCE AND ACCOUNTABILITY

yet, you will. It's the question that makes us all break out in a cold sweat. Because on the surface, it sounds reasonable. AI generates content in seconds. It creates mood boards in minutes. It drafts strategies while you're having your morning coffee. Surely that means cheaper, right? Here's what's actually happening when you use AI effectively: you're not just doing the same work faster. You're doing better work. You're exploring more creative territories. You're testing more strategic angles. You're refining ideas until they sing. Your clients aren't paying you to type. They never were. They're paying for the strategic thinking that shapes the brief. The creative judgement that selects the best concept from dozens of possibilities. The years of experience that spot the idea with real commercial potential. AI amplifies all of this. It doesn't replace it. Think of it this way: a Formula 1 driver doesn't become less valuable when they get a faster car. They become more valuable because they can perform at an even higher level.

What happens when technology genuinely makes something cheaper? At Cannes this year, I met the founder of an established European production company. Alongside their traditional commercial work, they'd developed a 16-person AI production team. They now offer three tiers: traditional shoots, hybrid productions mixing real footage with AI-generated B-roll, and fully AI-created films. Here's the interesting bit: their pure AI projects sell for a third of the cost of traditional productions. You'd expect lower margins, right? Wrong. They're actually more profitable on the AI work. Why? Because while everyone else is still figuring out prompts, they've become specialists in a field with few experts. Scarcity drives value, even in a cheaper market. It can pay to build expertise where others fear to tread. This production company didn't panic about AI threatening their business – they leaned into it, developed real capability and found themselves charging premium rates in what everyone assumed would be a commoditised market. Here are four ways to reframe the conversation:

1. **Show the iceberg:** When you present work to clients, show them what's beneath the surface. 'We explored eight different strategic directions using AI, then applied our expertise to identify the three with the strongest commercial potential. Here's why we selected this one.'

2. **Demonstrate quality gains:** Don't just tell them it's better – show them. Present side-by-side comparisons when appropriate. 'Here's what we would have delivered in the old world. Here's what we can deliver now with AI assisting us.'

3. **Position partnership:** Explain that you're not just using AI to serve them better today. You're building expertise that keeps your client ahead of their competitors tomorrow. While others are still figuring out prompts, they'll be leveraging AI for breakthrough campaigns.

4. **Be clear about your value:** Explain that, yes, AI helped you generate a mood board, but that you spent that saved time testing it with your client's target audience, refining the concept and exploring three alternative creative directions. The result isn't cheaper, it's actually better.

It's important you learn how to master this conversation. Agencies that let their clients accept the 'AI = cheaper' narrative will find themselves in a race to the bottom that nobody wins. Which conversation are you having with your clients?

Accountability: Keeping your roadmap on track

You've now come a long way. From the tentative first steps into the world of AI to mapping workflows, developing governance structures and crafting client communication strategies. Now comes perhaps the most challenging part of all: sustaining momentum and ensuring your roadmap doesn't gather dust alongside countless other promising initiatives.

Let's be clear: most agencies fail at the implementation stage. They create impressive plans, hold enthusiastic kick-off meetings, and then nothing happens. The day-to-day pressures of client work take over, and transformation efforts fade into the background. But this won't happen to you, because you're going to approach this with the same rigour you apply to client campaigns. Your AI taskforce isn't just a think tank, it's your implementation engine. Without clear accountability, even the most brilliant AI roadmap will stall. Here's the most common pattern: you've created your brilliant strategy, mapped out the initiatives and secured leadership buy-in. You're feeling pretty pleased with yourself. Then six months later, you realise nothing has actually happened. The reason is depressingly simple: you assigned tasks to 'the team' instead of actual human beings with names, deadlines and consequences. This isn't just an AI problem – it's human nature. When everyone is responsible, no one is responsible. When the deadline says Q2 instead of March 15th, it might as well say 'never'. The fix is brutally simple but requires discipline to implement consistently.

Every AI initiative needs an owner – not a department, not a committee, but a specific person. Someone who wakes up thinking about it, whose performance review depends on its success, who gets the credit when it works and faces the difficult conversation when it doesn't. Give them a clear brief, a realistic deadline and the authority to make decisions. Then get out of their way. Your AI transformation isn't a team sport; it's a collection of individual accountabilities that add up to something bigger. The most successful agencies build accountability into their AI journey from day one by naming specific owners for every initiative on their roadmap. This doesn't mean these people do all the work themselves, but they're unambiguously responsible for progress. They break longer initiatives into shorter phases with concrete deliverables, understanding that what gets measured gets done. They schedule standing meetings – weekly or monthly, never quarterly – specifically to review AI initiative progress, treating these check-ins with the same importance as client reviews. Most importantly, they make progress visible by displaying their AI roadmap where everyone can see it, with current status clearly tracked. This visibility creates peer accountability and prevents initiatives from quietly disappearing when other priorities emerge. Without this systematic approach to ownership and tracking, you're not creating a plan – you're creating a wish list that will join all the other abandoned strategic initiatives gathering dust on your shared drive.

Start small, learn fast

The agencies making the most impressive progress with AI aren't necessarily those with the biggest budgets or the most ambitious plans. They're the ones following a disciplined approach of starting small, learning quickly and gradually expanding their efforts. I spent half my career as a management consultant at Accenture and Q5, helping organisations change, and I've seen many organisations make the same mistake when implementing new systems or processes. They try to change everything at once. The result is always the same: overwhelm, confusion and very little actual progress. The ambitious transformation plan becomes an expensive lesson in what not to do.

The approach that actually works is deceptively simple: pick one thing, master it completely, then move to the next. If you're going to focus on AI-powered mood boards, spend the time to genuinely understand the tools, refine your process and measure the real impact. Don't move on until you can confidently say you've mastered that workflow and can demonstrate clear benefits. Once you've proven success in one area, you've built something far more valuable than an efficient mood board process – you've created a template for change. The same disciplines, the same learning approach, the same measurement framework can be applied to the next workflow, and the next. Six months of this disciplined approach will transform five key processes rather than failing to transform twenty. This isn't about limiting your ambition, it's about channelling it effectively. Every successful transformation I've been part of has followed this pattern: start focused, build competence, prove value, then scale. It might feel slower than your ambition wants, but it's infinitely faster than the alternative of trying everything and mastering nothing. The key is choosing your pilot projects with care. You want initiatives that are highly visible within your agency but which are manageable in scope. Success builds momentum, and momentum is what transforms sceptics into advocates. Pick something that matters but won't break the business if it goes wrong.

Document everything as you go. What prompts worked? Which tools delivered the best results? Where did you hit roadblocks? Capture these lessons in a central knowledge base that everyone can access. This isn't just for your benefit – it's building the institutional knowledge that will accelerate every subsequent AI initiative. Measure real impact, not vanity metrics. Yes, you might save two hours on mood board creation, but what did you do with those two hours? Did it enable better creative exploration? Higher-quality client presentations? More strategic thinking time? Track the meaningful changes, not just the obvious ones, and make your successes visible. When something works, celebrate it publicly within your agency. Share before-and-after examples. Highlight the team members who drove the success. Show sceptics what's possible when AI is implemented thoughtfully. Nothing converts doubters quite like seeing their colleagues thrive. This disciplined, step-by-step approach might feel slower than the grand transformation your ambition craves. However, it's the difference between actually changing how your agency works and creating an impressive slide deck for the board that then gathers dust.

Balancing innovation with reality

The real challenge in implementing your AI roadmap is that it's competing for attention with everything else that keeps your business running. Client deadlines don't pause for AI experiments. Resource constraints don't disappear because you've got a transformation plan. Unexpected challenges will always emerge at the worst possible moment. The agencies that move forward quickly with AI aren't the ones with the most time or the fewest distractions. They're the ones who've learned to weave AI progress into the fabric of how they already work, rather than treating it as some separate, special initiative that happens when everything else is quiet.

The breakthrough comes from a change of mindset: stop thinking of AI as an add-on to your business and start thinking of it as part of your business. When you incorporate AI progress updates into your regular team meetings, you're not creating more work – you're ensuring it stays visible and accountable. When you allocate dedicated time in people's schedules for AI initiatives, even during busy periods, you're saying this matters as much as client work. When you track AI initiatives in the same project management system you use for client work, you're treating them with the same seriousness. This integration approach works because it leverages systems and habits you've already established. Your team knows how to manage projects, attend meetings and hit deadlines. You don't need to teach them new behaviours – you just need to apply existing ones to AI initiatives.

The key is protecting the time while keeping it realistic. Yes, you need dedicated hours for AI work, but they don't need to be massive blocks. Two hours a week consistently will achieve more than a sporadic day a month. Yes, you need to budget genuine resources – time, money, training – but you don't need to transform your entire operation overnight. The most successful AI implementations I've seen balance quick wins that demonstrate immediate value with longer-term goals that create lasting change. Remember: your AI roadmap isn't competing for time with running your business. When done right, it becomes an integral part of it.

Building for the future

In all of this, it's still possible to lose sight of the big picture. Don't just plan for what AI can do today. AI development is moving at breakneck speed. The tools you're learning today will have moved on within three months, and within twelve months will be capable of completely new things. By the time you've mastered this generation of AI, the next wave will make your workflows look quaint. It becomes important to evaluate, adopt and take advantage of new technologies as they emerge. Organisations that do this will be the ones who've built organisational muscles for technological adoption that work regardless of what specific tool appears next.

The creative industry is experiencing more disruption than at any point since the consumer internet hit the scene in the late 1990s, except this time it will be faster. By following the structured roadmap approach outlined in this book, you're building that same muscle in your organisation. You're creating a foundation that will allow you to respond quickly to technological shifts while competitors scramble to understand new developments. You'll have established processes for evaluation and adoption that work whether the next breakthrough is in video generation, voice synthesis, website development or something we haven't even imagined yet. You're learning to scale successful innovations consistently, moving from successful pilots to agency-wide implementation with confidence. Your technology adoption becomes aligned with your business strategy, reinforcing your agency's unique strengths and competitive positioning rather than chasing every shiny new tool that appears.

Both employees and clients are increasingly drawn to agencies with sophisticated approaches to emerging technologies. They want to work with organisations that embrace change rather than fear it, that see technological disruptions as opportunities rather than threats. The agency landscape of 2030 and beyond will look dramatically different from today's. The question isn't whether change is coming – it's who will navigate it most effectively.

The systematic roadmap you've developed, the accountability structures you've established, and the governance frameworks you've created aren't just about today's AI tools. They're building your agency's capacity to thrive amid constant change – to turn technological disruption from a threat into your greatest competitive advantage. When the next wave of AI capabilities arrives, and it will, you'll be ready. Not because you predicted exactly what it would look like, but because you built an organisation capable of adapting to whatever comes next.

Key takeaways

- **Governance isn't bureaucracy, it's your competitive safety net.** Clear AI policies enable bold experimentation within defined boundaries, building your clients' trust while protecting your business from avoidable risks.

- **Clients' perspectives span a wide spectrum.** Perspectives range from complete AI rejection to enthusiastic adoption, requiring tailored communication strategies that address specific concerns rather than generic explanations.

- **Transparency transforms potential friction into competitive advantage.** Agencies that openly discuss their AI approach, limitations and governance build significantly stronger relationships with clients than those who avoid the conversation.

- **The 'AI equals cheaper' trap destroys value.** Reframe efficiency conversations around enhanced exploration, better quality and expanded creative possibilities rather than accepting downward price pressure.

- **Accountability requires named owners.** Every AI initiative needs a specific person responsible for progress, not committees or departments that diffuse responsibility.

- **Start small and prove value systematically.** Mastering one AI workflow completely creates a template for scaling success rather than attempting everything simultaneously and achieving nothing.

- **Regular review prevents roadmap drift.** Scheduled check-ins, progress visibility and course corrections keep AI transformation moving forward despite competing daily pressures.

GOVERNANCE AND ACCOUNTABILITY

Your action point: Lock in your accountability system

Spend twenty minutes setting up the infrastructure to keep your AI roadmap on track. First, identify one specific person (with their name, not a department) as the owner for each AI initiative you've identified. Second, schedule a recurring thirty-minute check-in every month specifically to review AI progress – treat these as seriously as client meetings. Finally, choose one visible location (physical board, shared document or project management tool) where everyone can see current AI initiative status and progress. This simple accountability infrastructure will prevent your AI transformation from becoming another abandoned strategic plan, ensuring consistent momentum regardless of daily pressures.

13
Where is all this going?

Trying to predict what happens next with AI feels a bit like standing on a railway platform watching the 6:43 to London approach at 150 mph. You know it's coming, you can feel the ground trembling, but the sheer scale and speed of it makes you slightly queasy. The technology is evolving so fast that I can barely wrap my head around what might be possible two years from now, let alone five. However, there are patterns emerging from the chaos, and if you're running a creative business right now, you need to understand what's bearing down on you. What 'good' looks like is about to change completely, and I don't mean doing the same work faster – I mean reimagining what creative work can be.

Beyond faster and cheaper

Have a look at a screenshot of Amazon's website from 1996 – there are plenty of images online. Look at it properly for a moment. I started my first office job that year, and remember this quite well. Back then, this was cutting-edge, state-of-the-art web design that would have cost hundreds of thousands, and taken experienced software engineers months to build. Today? My nephew could build something better in his bedroom in twenty minutes simply by talking to ChatGPT. You couldn't charge a penny for it because it's laughably basic. Here's what's fascinating: you can still charge hundreds of thousands for a website today. What's completely changed is what constitutes a 'website'. It's now a rich brand expression, a complex piece of software, an entire digital ecosystem. The goalposts moved, and those who moved with them prospered.

AI is about to do exactly the same thing to our industry. The work you've been creating for the last five years? It's going to look as quaint as that Amazon homepage. Not because it's bad work, but because the possibilities are about to explode beyond recognition. The way to stay relevant isn't to defend what you're doing now; it's to grab these tools and see how far they can take you. The state of the art is changing, and you need to change with it. As a proportion of US GDP, there is more investment behind generative AI than there was behind the Apollo programme that put humans on the moon. It's nothing less than the largest technological undertaking in human history. When that much money and brain power get focused on something, remarkable things happen fast. The models themselves are already excellent, and getting better every month. However, everything's also about to become fluid. Text, image, video, sound, music – these artificial boundaries we've built our careers around are dissolving. The machines are learning to think across all these formats simultaneously, switching between them as naturally as you'd switch between speaking and writing.

Your new celebrity workforce

Think about what this can unlock. Imagine walking into Decathlon and Rafa Nadal helps you choose your perfect tennis racket. Not a recording, but an interactive avatar on a video screen (and eventually a hologram) that asks about your playing style, your experience, your budget (and your backhand weakness), and points you to the right racket for you. He's having the same conversation with 500 other people in other stores around the world simultaneously. Simon Schama becomes your personal history tutor, adjusting his teaching style to match your learning pace. You watch the football with Lionel Messi providing commentary tailored to your level of knowledge of the game. You decide to spend Friday night in with a glass of wine, chatting with Joey, Chandler and the rest of the cast of *Friends*. Anna Wintour becomes your personal stylist, helping you pick out the right threads for that big event. You watch the latest *Mission Impossible* thriller, but instead of Tom Cruise in the lead role, it's you.

Not only will your clients want to create experiences like these, but you'll want to create them for your agency, too. Imagine briefing David Droga on your campaign strategy in real time, or having Paula Scher critique your brand identity as you develop it. Picture presenting concepts to a board that includes virtual versions of your client's customers, each responding with authentic reactions based on deep research into their demographic. What brand wouldn't want their spokesperson available 24/7, speaking personally to every customer, never having a bad day or saying the wrong thing? What agency wouldn't want access to the greatest creative minds in history as collaborative partners? This all feels a bit like science fiction, but in reality it's not that far away.

The age of personal AI assistants

The models are not only getting better, they are getting smaller, too. Soon, a sophisticated AI will run on your phone, or on your smart glasses, with no need to connect to the internet. Once that happens, they can operate with almost zero latency, and, crucially, your data stays private because it's not being uploaded to the cloud. This creates the trust necessary for AI to become truly personal. Once you give an AI access to your email, it knows what you do for work and who your colleagues are, as well as everything you have ever bought online and where you bought it from. Once it has access to your WhatsApp it knows who your friends are, and once it has access to your calendar, it knows who you meet and where you go.

Not only that, AI models are becoming capable of interacting online. In July 2025, OpenAI released ChatGPT Agent Mode – a semi-autonomous agent that can control a website and conduct activities online on your behalf. Imagine personal digital assistants that can see what you see, hear what you hear, work online and give you advice, commentary and conversation whenever you want it. Your AI agent is going to become your digital butler, and this shift will transform how commerce works. For low-involvement purchases, your agent will just sort it out. Running low on dishwasher tablets? Done. Need to book a dentist appointment? Handled. Want the best deal on car insurance? Sorted while you sleep. However, for the big decisions – buying a house, choosing a car, planning a wedding – people will still want to be deeply involved. These become human experiences, emotional journeys that no algorithm can replicate. Marketing will need to adapt to both worlds – creating engaging in-person experiences, and optimising for automated agent-driven commerce.

This fundamental shift splits the market in two: brands selling to agents (price-focused, efficiency-driven) and brands selling to humans (experience-focused, emotion-driven). Many will find themselves in the middle, needing to do both. The strategies for each will be completely different, and whether you're in performance marketing, brand activation or creative design, these technologies will change what clients want from you. Think about how this changes your agency's relationship with them. When their customers' agents are making routine purchasing decisions based purely on rational criteria, how does brand loyalty work? How do you create emotional connections with algorithms? Conversely, when human decisions become more considered and deliberate, how do you create experiences worthy of that attention?

Three roads diverging

I can see three distinct paths emerging for creative work, and the choice you make will determine not just your survival, but your success:

- **The volume game:** Agencies that use AI to pump out vast quantities of content. Cheap, cheerful, good enough. They'll compete on price and speed and need massive scale to succeed. They will essentially become creative technology companies selling platforms to their clients. Think content farms, but with better production values.

- **The innovation players:** This is where the smart money goes. Using AI to create experiences that weren't possible before. Pushing boundaries. Making things that make people stop and stare and share. This is where you want to be. Imagine campaigns that adapt in real time to individual viewers, or brand experiences that remember every interaction a customer has ever had. Picture creative concepts that can be tested with thousands of variations before a single pound is spent on production.

- **The craft defenders:** Hand-made, provably human, artisanal creative work. Like vinyl records in a Spotify world – beautiful, premium, but serving a small market willing to pay significantly more for the story behind the work.

The middle path offers the most opportunity because it combines the power of AI with the insight and creativity that clients actually value. However, choosing this path means you can't just use AI to do what you've always done – you need to reimagine what's possible.

From campaigns to creative engines

Perhaps the most profound disruption is to the concept of the 'campaign' itself. The campaign model assumes fixed creative assets distributed through pre-planned channels for a defined period. However, AI enables something fundamentally different: continuously generated, personalised creative output that adapts in real time to individual contexts. Why create a single YouTube ad when you could create a system that generates thousands of personalised videos? Why design three variations of a print ad when you could create dynamic visuals that evolve based on location, weather conditions and local events? This shift from fixed assets to generative systems requires completely different capabilities. Instead of executing specific creative visions, you'll need to design frameworks within which AI can generate brand-appropriate content autonomously. Imagine a system that automatically creates hundreds of personalised social posts daily, each optimised for specific audience segments while maintaining perfect brand consistency. Or retail experiences that adapt their visual language, messaging and product recommendations based on everything from weather patterns to trending topics. Your creative brief won't describe a single campaign – it'll define the parameters within which thousands of creative variants can emerge. You become the architect of creative possibility rather than the executor of individual ideas.

The death of the project-based model

This transformation demands more than new tools – it requires fundamentally rethinking how you structure and price your work. Most agencies still operate on a project basis: brief in, work done, invoice sent. AI undermines this model in profound ways. When creating 100 variations costs the same as creating one, how do you price that work? When an asset can continually evolve based on real-time data, when does a 'project' ever truly end? The economics that have sustained agencies for decades – charging for time and materials – are rapidly becoming obsolete. Why would clients pay agency rates for work that, from their perspective, seems increasingly automated?

The solution isn't to charge less for the same deliverables. It's to redefine what your agency sells. You're moving from creating campaigns to building creative systems. From delivering finished work to providing ongoing creative capability. Consider what's emerging: outcome-based pricing, where you tie fees to measurable business results – performance components tied to campaign metrics, revenue-sharing models for ecommerce projects, or success fees for achieving specific business objectives. Platform as a service approaches where you build and maintain custom AI creative platforms for clients on a subscription basis – brand-specific image generation systems trained on a client's visual identity, or dynamic content adaptation engines that personalise messaging across channels.

Think about what R/GA did with Nike. Rather than just creating campaigns, they built NIKEiD, a platform that allowed customers to design their own shoes. This type of platform-building approach will become standard in the AI era. You're not just serving clients – you're building the infrastructure that serves their customers.

Your org chart is obsolete

We're going to see new roles emerge in your agency. People who think like artists but understand technology well enough to coax magic from machines. Creative technologists who can bridge the gap between 'Wouldn't it be amazing if...' and 'Actually, we can do that'. I watched this happen in photography when digital arrived. Suddenly, every shoot needed a digital tech – someone who understood both the creative vision and the technical possibilities. They became invaluable because they could translate between worlds. That's happening again, right now, in every creative discipline. These aren't just technical roles – they're strategic positions that will help you win pitches, solve clients' problems and create work that competitors can't match. Start identifying these people in your team now, or start looking for them. They'll be worth their weight in gold. Think about how this changes your hiring strategy, too. Are you still looking for people who can execute perfectly within established parameters? Or are you seeking those who can imagine new parameters entirely? Your next hire isn't a designer or a copywriter. It's someone who can help you build AI into the way you design and write. The agencies that adapt their talent strategy fastest will have a significant advantage.

The Netflix test

Ted Sarandos, Netflix's CEO, was recently asked by investors how he planned to use AI to make films cheaper. His response was perfect: 'Customers don't want films that are cheaper. They want films that are better.'[35] Most of your clients think the same way. Sure, they'll take savings where they can get them, but what they really want is results that move the needle. Give them that and they will pay the earth. This is the conversation that separates the agencies that thrive from those that merely survive. You're not selling automation – you're selling transformation.

AI can do a lot of things, but it can't yet have that moment of insight that changes everything. It can't spot the pattern that everyone else missed. It can't connect two unrelated ideas in a way that makes people slap their foreheads and say, 'Why didn't I think of that?' Mike Cessario, the founder of Liquid Death, saw a rockstar drinking water from an energy drink can to avoid looking uncool on stage.[36] One observation led to a billion-dollar brand. AI didn't create that insight – a human being did, by being present in the world and understanding how people really think and feel. Gymshark interviewed 500 gym enthusiasts and discovered they had a name for the uncomfortable times your shorts ride up after squats: 'squat crack'. One killer insight led to campaigns that spoke directly to their audience's real experience. AI isn't going to give you moments like that. Your job is to have brilliant ideas and then use every tool available – including AI – to bring them to life in ways that weren't possible before. The insight remains human; the execution becomes superhuman.

Becoming the creative director of everything

AI turns you into a creative director of your own expanded capabilities. You still need brilliant ideas. You still need to know what good looks like. But now you're briefing a tireless team that never sleeps, never has creative blocks and can explore hundreds of directions while you focus on the strategic thinking. Think of it like directing a film. You don't operate every camera or paint every set, but your vision guides every decision. AI becomes your crew – endlessly capable, waiting for direction, ready to make your ideas reality. The craft isn't disappearing – it's evolving. Your job becomes preserving creative intent throughout the process, making sure the final work tells the story you want to tell. Success won't come from having the best technology – it'll come from having the best ideas about how to use it. However, this evolution demands new skills from you and your team. You need to become fluent in directing machines, not just people. You need to understand what AI can and can't do so you can brief it effectively. Most importantly, you need to maintain creative control even when the tools become incredibly sophisticated.

What this means for your agency

We're living through the biggest transformation in creative work since the invention of the printing press. Yes, some skills will become obsolete, but new opportunities are opening up just as fast as old ones are closing down. Think about what happened when everyone got access to digital cameras and Photoshop. Did photography die? Did design become worthless? No – the industry exploded. There are more photographers, designers and filmmakers working today than ever before. The market grew because suddenly everyone needed more visual content. AI is going to do the same thing for your industry. Instead of one campaign, brands will want hundreds – each tailored to micro-audiences. Instead of static content, they'll want dynamic experiences that adapt in real time. Instead of guessing what works, they'll want systems that learn and improve continuously.

This means your client relationships will evolve, too. You'll move from being a service provider to being a strategic partner.

Instead of delivering finished campaigns, you might build creative systems that generate ongoing content. Instead of periodic projects, you could develop continuous optimisation partnerships. The pitching process will transform as well. Imagine being able to show your clients not just concepts, but working prototypes of AI-driven campaigns. Picture being able to demonstrate, in real time, how your creative approach would perform across different demographics and channels. The agencies that can do this will have an enormous advantage. Your pricing conversations will become more sophisticated too. Instead of justifying hourly rates, you'll be discussing the value of creative systems that work 24/7, personalising content for millions of customers simultaneously. You'll move from selling campaigns to licensing creative intelligence.

In five years' time, you'll look back at how you work today the same way you look back at that Amazon homepage from 1996 – with fond nostalgia for simpler times, but with deep gratitude for how much more you can achieve now. The agencies that embrace this transformation won't just survive – they'll create a new standard for what creative work can be. They'll build deeper relationships with their clients, solve bigger problems and create work that actually moves the needle in ways that were previously impossible.

Your creative work will become more impactful, not less. Your strategic thinking will become more valuable, not redundant. Your relationship with clients will become deeper, not more transactional. Your next creative brief could be the beginning of something extraordinary. Your next client conversation could open up possibilities neither of you had imagined. Your next hire could be the person who helps you bridge the gap between where you are and where you could be.

The future belongs to those who build it, not those who wait for it to arrive. The good news? You're already building it, one experiment, one project, one brilliant idea at a time.

Postscript: How I used AI to help me write this book

This wouldn't be a very convincing book about how agencies should adopt AI if I wasn't using AI tools myself. Just as I encourage you to be transparent about your use of AI, here is an explanation of my process. I think it also helps illuminate some of the concepts in the book.

The premise and thinking behind the book already existed, in the form of Spark's AI training and consultancy: our AI Fundamentals workshops, Leadership workshops and groundbreaking AI Accelerator programme. These are the culmination of two and a half years spent learning about and using AI myself, thinking and talking with others about how AI will transform agencies, and bouncing ideas off Spark's many brilliant collaborators and clients. It is also a good example of how to interact with an LLM (Chapter 5). I used my own thoughts to direct the AI, and then used my own thoughts to edit what came out. The final copy is a mixture of copy I wrote myself, and AI-generated copy I then edited myself, and I'm sure there are some AI-generated paragraphs that have survived unscathed.

The result? I feel this falls firmly into the augmentation camp (Chapter 9) rather than automation or innovation. The first draft of the book, some 50,000 words, was completed in about fifteen days. I then read through it in full and made numerous manual edits for a further ten days to create a final draft. I moved between Google Notebook, a ChatGPT Project and a Claude Project. I would frequently ask the AI to help me rephrase or add more interest to a paragraph. I then asked friends, colleagues and clients to read and suggest improvements.

How does this compare to the pre-AI process of writing a book? Well, I've never written a book before, so I don't have a good control to measure against. However, using AI to help me has certainly given me more time to think about the structure and flow of the book, ensuring it is as practical and accessible as possible, while not dumbing down the content in any way. It has also been a huge help to someone who is full of ideas and thoughts, but is better at speaking than writing. Therefore, it has helped turn a non-author into an author – another example of the broadening of roles explored earlier, and by Stephen Pretorius in Chapter 3. It has also deepened my skill at using AI (specifically Notebook, ChatGPT and Claude). I was already extremely proficient (I teach AI use for a living), but interacting constantly with it on a single task over many days gives you a level of nuance and understanding of its strengths and weaknesses that is hard to obtain any other way.

I hope this helps give a practical example of AI augmentation in action. Did it help create a better outcome than if I had written the book on my own? Yes. Did it speed up the process? Also, yes. Did it reduce the time to close to zero? Absolutely not. Does the fact that I used AI to create it reduce the value of this book to you, the client? Only you can answer that, but I'm fairly sure it didn't.

Notes

1 Ipsos presentation 'Misfits vs. Machines' at Most Contagious London, 28 November 2024
2 T Mucci, *The History of AI* (IBM, undated), www.ibm.com/think/topics/history-of-artificial-intelligence, accessed 31 July 2025
3 A Vaswani, N Shazeer, N Parmar, J Uszkoreit, L Jones, AN Gomez, Ł Kaiser and I Polosukhin, 'Attention is all you need', *Advances in Neural Information Processing Systems*, 30 (2017), 5998–6008, https://dl.acm.org/doi/10.5555/3295222.3295349, accessed 28 August 2025
4 GE Moore, 'Cramming more components onto integrated circuits', *Electronics*, 38/8 (1965), 114–117, https://ieeexplore.ieee.org/document/4785860, accessed 25 August 2025
5 S Ambler, *Large Language Models (LLMs) Hallucinate 100% of the Time* (Scott Ambler, 2024), https://scottambler.com/llms-always-hallucinate, accessed 30 July 2025

6   Ipsos presentation 'Misfits vs. Machines' at Most Contagious London, 28 November 2024
7   Publicis Groupe, *Full Year 2023 Results* (Publicis Groupe, 2024), www.publicisgroupe.com/sites/default/files/press-releases/2024-02/CP_Resultats_FY2023%20GB.pdf, accessed 30 July 2025
8   R Rajamannar, 'How AI could change the advertising business' (2025), www.youtube.com/watch?v=CKh2qcz1K4M, accessed 30 July 2025
9   R Rajamannar, 'How AI could change the advertising business' (2025), www.youtube.com/watch?v=CKh2qcz1K4M, accessed 30 July 2025
10 LBB, *Always the Real Thing? Coca-Cola AI-generates Classic Christmas Ad* (Little Black Book, 2024), https://lbbonline.com/news/coca-cola-ai-christmas-ad-holidays-are-coming-2024, accessed 30 July 2025
11 r/singularity, 'Coca-Cola releases annual Christmas commercial fully AI generated' (2024), www.reddit.com/r/singularity/comments/1gs976j/coca_cola_releases_annual_christmas_commercial, accessed 30 July 2025
12 J Pattisall, 'Coca-Cola's AI-generated holiday ads approach a creative tipping point' (Forrester, 2024), www.forrester.com/blogs/coca-colas-ai-generated-holiday-ads-approach-a-creative-tipping-point, accessed 31 July 2025
13 Naomi Joshi, 'The quality makers: Diarra Bousso of DIARRABLU', Naomi Joshi's blog (6 June 2025), www.naomishefalijoshi.com/stories/the-quality-makers-diarra-bousso-of-diarrablu, accessed 11 August 2025
14 B Fischer, 'How Diarra Bousso turned her love of math into a formula-driven fashion brand', (Fashionista, 27 November 2023), https://fashionista.com/2023/11/diarrablu-diarra-bousso-designer-career-interview-2023, accessed 11 August 2025

NOTES

15 GS Vierek, 'What life means to Einstein', *Saturday Evening Post* (26 October 1929)

16 See https://theresanaiforthat.com

17 A Karpathy (@karpathy) 'The hottest new programming language is English' (24 January 2023), https://x.com/karpathy/status/1617979122625712128?lang=fa, accessed 30 July 2025

18 WPP, *WPP announces investment in Stability AI and new partnership to shape the future of media and entertainment production* (WPP, 2025), www.wpp.com/en/news/2025/03/wpp-announces-investment-in-stability-ai, accessed 30 July 2025

19 Weber (@weberwongwong) 'FLORA (@florafaunaai) raised our seed round...' (28 May 2025), https://x.com/weberwongwong/status/1927756769238905083, accessed 30 July 2025

20 US Copyright Office, *Copyright and Artificial Intelligence* (undated), www.copyright.gov/ai, accessed 30 July 2025

21 Policy and Evidence Centre, *AI, Intellectual Property and Regulation* (PEC, 2024), https://pec.ac.uk/intellectual-property-and-regulation, accessed 30 July 2025

22 UK Intellectual Property Office, *Copyright and AI: Consultation* (UK IPO, 2024), www.gov.uk/government/consultations/copyright-and-artificial-intelligence/copyright-and-artificial-intelligence, accessed 30 July 2025

23 IT Pereira, 'ChatGPT, Deepseek & Co: How much energy do AI-powered chatbots consume?', *euronews* (17 March 2025), www.euronews.com/my-europe/2025/03/17/chatgpt-deepseek-co-how-much-energy-do-ai-powered-chatbots-consume, accessed 31 July 2025

24 International Energy Agency, *Energy Demand From AI* (IEA, 2024), www.iea.org/reports/energy-and-ai/energy-demand-from-ai, accessed 30 July 2025

25 Smartly.ai, *What Is the CO2 Emission Per ChatGPT Query?* (Smartly.ai, 2024), https://smartly.ai/blog/the-carbon-footprint-of-chatgpt-how-much-co2-does-a-query-generate, accessed 31 July 2025

26 H Ritchie, *What's the Carbon Footprint of Using ChatGPT?* (Sustainability by numbers, 2025), www.sustainabilitybynumbers.com/p/carbon-footprint-chatgpt, accessed 31 July 2025

27 R Frost, 'ChatGPT "drinks" a bottle of fresh water for every 20 to 50 questions we ask, study warns', *euronews* (20 April 2023), www.euronews.com/green/2023/04/20/chatgpt-drinks-a-bottle-of-fresh-water-for-every-20-to-50-questions-we-ask-study-warns, accessed 31 July 2025

28 J Morrison, C Na, J Fernandez, T Dettmers, E Strubell and J Dodge, *Holistically Evaluating the Environmental Impact of Creating Language Models* (Cornell University, 2025), https://arxiv.org/abs/2503.05804, accessed 31 July 2025

29 IT Pereira, 'ChatGPT, Deepseek & Co: How much energy do AI-powered chatbots consume?', *euronews* (17 March 2025), www.euronews.com/my-europe/2025/03/17/chatgpt-deepseek-co-how-much-energy-do-ai-powered-chatbots-consume, accessed 31 July 2025

30 Spark AI, *AI in Creative Agencies 2025* (*Spark AI*, 2025), www.wearespark.ai/ai-creative-agencies-2025, accessed 30 July 2025

31 Hargreaves Lansdown, *RWS Holdings PLC*, www.hl.co.uk/shares/shares-search-results/r/rws-holdings-plc-ordinary-1p, accessed 30 July 2025

32 The Economist, 'What ChatGPT's corporate victims have in common', *The Economist* (20 November 2024), www.economist.com/business/2024/11/20/what-chatgpts-corporate-victims-have-in-common, accessed 13 August 2025

NOTES

33 Spark AI, *AI in Creative Agencies 2025* (Spark AI, 2025), www.wearespark.ai/ai-creative-agencies-2025, accessed 30 July 2025

34 S Betts, 'The question isn't "if" we should embrace AI anymore; it's "how well" we implement it', LinkedIn, www.linkedin.com/posts/seanbetts_omguk-artificialintelligence-generativeai-activity-7307359616655347716-LCCx, accessed 13 August 2025

35 A D'Alessandro, 'Netflix boss Ted Sarandos pours cold water on *New York Times*' report that Dan Lin wants to make movies "Better, cheaper and less frequent"', *Deadline* (18 April 2024), https://deadline.com/2024/04/netflix-ted-sarandos-dan-lin-1235889649, accessed 30 July 2025

36 T Huddleston Jr and Z Green, 'How Liquid Death's 40-year-old founder turned "the dumbest name" and a Facebook post into a $700 million water brand', CNBC (26 November 2022), www.cnbc.com/2022/11/26/liquid-death-ceo-mike-cessario-we-chose-the-dumbest-possible-name-for-water.html?msockid=0f18d3f9fc5b63e00a8cc5e8fdf6621c, accessed 30 July 2025

Acknowledgements

This book wouldn't exist without the support and generosity of many people.

First and foremost, my business partner – and wife – Emma Wharton Love. Without her, this book wouldn't just be unfinished, it wouldn't have been started. Amid the whirlwind of building a startup, she helped me carve out the time and focus to write. She's read, refined and improved every section, and the way we think and talk about AI is the result of a shared vision for the future of creative businesses.

I'm also hugely grateful to those who've helped shape my thinking through conversations, interviews and shared experiences. In particular: my good friend Ben Rickard at Dragonfly, Kate Ross at eight&four, Perry Haydn-Taylor at Big Fish, Stu Tallis at Taxi, Morten Legarth at VCCP Faith and Rahul Malhotra at Shell. Your insights and openness have been invaluable.

Thank you, too, to the brilliant people who help us deliver AI transformation at Spark: Steve Edwards, Emma Jackson, Alicia Grimes, Simone Carasco, Matthew Maxwell, Mette Davis, Jonas Haefele and Anya Turk. Your thinking and collaboration have made our work better – and more fun. And to members of our advisory board I haven't yet mentioned: Priya Guha MBE and Sofia Pires; thank you for helping us keep looking up and out.

Next, a thank you to the people whose writing and speaking on AI continues to influence and inspire: Ethan Mollick, Paul Roetzer, Mike Kaput, Benedict Evans, Rory Flynn, Luka Tisler, Bryan Sykes, and many more I'll inevitably forget to mention.

And finally, a huge thank you to all the agencies that have chosen to work with Spark AI over the last eighteen months. We have learned at least as much from you as you have from us.

The Author

Jules Love is the co-founder of Spark AI, a UK-based training and consulting company that helps creative agencies and marketing teams embrace generative AI. Since launching in 2024, the Spark team has grown to ten people and worked with over fifty creative businesses, from branding agencies to global in-house teams.

Everything in this book is based on Spark's AI Fundamentals and AI Accelerator programmes, and it's not just theory – it's been honed by the experience of seeing what really works with their clients.

Jules's career bridges the worlds of creativity and technology. Since studying Physics and Art at A-level, he has been fascinated with both logic and imagination. That dual focus has remained a thread throughout his working life: first as a strategy consultant with Accenture and Q5, then as a successful advertising photographer and director working with top agencies and household-name brands across the globe.

Since discovering Midjourney in 2022 he's studied Applied Generative AI at MIT, lectures on AI strategy at Oxford's Saïd Business School, and regularly speaks at events including The AI Summit, Agency Hackers and Building Brands. He was recently a judge for the Association of Photographers Awards and was named one of the 100 most influential people in UK digital and tech by BIMA in June 2025.

Learn more about Spark's AI Accelerator Programme at **wearespark.ai**

Follow Jules online at **linkedin.com/in/juleslove**

Get a bi-weekly drop of what's new in Creative AI at **wearespark.ai/spark-intelligence-ai-newsletter-for-creative-industries**